AT PEACE WITH FAILURE

AT PEACE WITH FAILURE

Duane Mehl

AUGSBURG Publishing House • Minneapolis

AT PEACE WITH FAILURE

Copyright © 1984 Augsburg Publishing House

All rights reserved. Except for brief quotations in critical articles or reviews, no part of this book may be reproduced in any manner without prior written permission from the publisher. Write to: Permissions, Augsburg Publishing House, 426 S. Fifth St., Box 1209, Minneapolis, MN 55440.

Scripture quotations unless otherwise noted are from the Holy Bible: New International Version. Copyright 1978 by the New York International Bible Society. Used by permission of Zondervan Bible Publishers.

Library of Congress Cataloging in Publication Data

Mehl, Duane.

At Peace with Failure.

1. Mehl, Duane. 2. Converts—United States—Biography. 3. Alcoholics—United States—Biography 4. Christian life—1960-   I. Title.
BV4935.M44A33   1984   248'.092'4   [B]   83-72114
ISBN 0-8066-2058-7 (pbk.)

Manufactured in the U.S.A.   APH 10-0472

1 2 3 4 5 6 7 8 9 0 1 2 3 4 5 6 7 8 9

To Les
comrade in mortal combat

Contents

	Preface	9
1	Failure	12
2	The Turning Point	17
3	Why Bad Things Will Always Happen to All People	22
4	How Therapy Fails Us	28
5	Waiting for God	35
6	The Last God on Earth	42
7	The God for Failures	51
8	God's Strength for Our Weakness	58
9	What Do You Deserve in Life?	63
10	Spiritual Exercise	69
11	Living with Loss	76
12	Why Resentment Is the Chief Offender	84
13	Living with Failure	92
14	Faith beyond Failure	103

Preface

During my lifetime I have experienced losses and have failed myself and others. At critical moments in my youthful and middle years, I lost loved ones within my immediate family circle. Because of a political battle in the church body I serve, I lost my primary vocation as a professor of Christian theology at a well-known seminary. Since that time, because of the tight job market, I have not even tried to find a comparable position.

I succumbed to alcoholism, and by God's grace and power I have at present recovered sobriety. During my drinking days, however, I managed to discourage my family and friends, my employer, and my community.

During most of my adult life I resisted any realistic resolution of my problems. I preferred to remain resentful over what I thought were the failures of others toward me. In the face of losses over which I had little control, I responded with self-pity guaranteed to keep me in a state of gnawing grief on the inside and malicious resentment on the outside.

Some years ago I realized that I needed a different approach to my problems. I felt that I had to find an entirely new way of living or else go crazy.

I read widely in the writings of various counselors, both secular and religious, hoping to find relief and power for my life. I read "experts" with such widely different perspectives as St. Francis and Wayne Dyer. The experience of reading *The Franciscan Rule* and *Your Erroneous Zones* back-to-back resulted, however, in more confusion than health.

I also visited professional therapists and talked to good friends who seemed to possess a therapeutic perspective. From them I learned that I "discounted" my potential and refused to "confront" my problems. I was told that I did not accept either myself or others as "OK."

I also learned that I did not practice "positive thinking," or even "possibility thinking." I did not "take charge" of my life, my counselors said. Apparently I did not believe, with Dyer, that "the sky is the limit," and when trying to "pull my own strings" I created nothing but a tangle—or at best a cat's cradle.

Without fully knowing it, I was searching in failure for a real God who no longer seemed to occupy the culture in which I lived. The problem of finding God in a society that seems to allow no space for God is at the heart of this book.

The clue to resolving this problem is painfully simple: We can never find God at all: *God finds us.* Precisely when we despair of helping ourselves, God can finally begin to help us in our times of great need.

God, I believe, responded to my needs. In this book

I hope to describe my experiences of loss and failure and the means by which God responded to me. I hope that these pages will also help those with similar difficulties to believe in a God who brings peace even in the midst of failure and loss.

1 • Failure

For many years I considered myself a failure. Most of that time I was an isolated and lonely failure. I thought almost everyone around me was a success. Everyone else seemed to have gained more than they had lost in life. Deep down inside I felt I was a catastrophe.

When I began some years ago to read success books by people such as Wayne Dyer, Jess Lair, and Robert Schuller, I often asked myself, "What could they really know about the failures and losses that they encouraged me to surmount?" After all, they had all become successful.

Jess Lair, I knew, had a heart attack at age 40. He then switched from advertising, which he hated, to teaching psychology, which he loved. He also wrote books that sold like popcorn at a matinee. I knew what that meant. Jess Lair had become a success through failure. He no longer knew what failure really felt like.

I knew, however, that I had experienced real losses and failure in life and knew what they felt like. I lost two brothers during my adolescence. One had died of a sudden and traumatic illness. The other died at age seven of a brain injury sustained at birth. I do not even like to recall the memories of those gruesome years.

When my first brother died, I felt both bereaved and overwhelmingly angry. I believed that God had let me down. Like Job, I thought God was treating me unfairly. Though I must have heard something about Christ's suffering and resurrection—perhaps at the funeral—I didn't see any relationship between those events and my own experience.

After my brother died, a close relative said to me, "God took your little brother because he had a tendency to lie. If he had grown up, he might have gone to hell."

Looking back on this remark, I am surprised that I didn't feel shocked by it at the time. Instead, I became worried that God would also take me—and for the same reason.

My father said little after my brother's death, but seemed to withdraw into his work. I'm not sure that I fully knew my father after that time. In response to my brother's death, he may have become a typical workaholic minister. Later I would follow in my father's footsteps and become compulsive with work, art, and, above all, with the pursuit of status. I would feel that I had to produce through success that which I had lost.

Shortly after my brothers' deaths, my parents moved from a small town in Kansas to a smaller town in Louisiana, and then to Chicago. There I became catatonic, but unable to close my eyes. For a whole year I stumbled around, terribly drowsy, but unable to fall asleep until 6:30 A.M., when I was supposed to get up for school.

I studied for spelling tests, but nodded off in the middle of words such as *indefatigable*. I took piano lessons at a music conservatory and gave recitals. But once while playing the climactic closing movement of Rachmaninoff's "Prelude in C-Sharp Minor," I froze into a solid state. As writers would say, I left the bells of Moscow "twisting in the wind."

Fortunately, I broke my arm playing high school basketball, and thus could give up my music scholarship at the conservatory. For the sake of the record, however, I achieved no successes at basketball either. Once, during a regional high school tournament, I stole the ball at half court and dribbled artfully down the floor for an easy lay-up, which I lofted from the free-throw line. The ball caromed off the backboard and hit me in the face. The entire crowd, including my mother, laughed at me. My poor coach benched me, telling me I was too nervous for this level of competition.

By age 18 I had become nervous about any kind of competition. I felt myself to be a failure at everything, because I had earlier lost my bearings in life.

Vocational Decisions

I had decided, however, when I was quite young that I would follow in the steps of my father and become a pastor. Since I was the oldest male child, that seemed like the natural thing to do. I gave no thought to emotional or intellectual qualifications for ministry. I was concerned, primarily, I think, with achieving my father's social status. Vince Lombardi used to say, "Winning isn't everything. It's the *only* thing." As I moved into my adult years in a secular world, I came close to destroying myself with that attitude.

In college I competed with others as an athlete, lover, actor, piano player, writer, student, and all-around pain in the neck. My friends and enemies assured me that I succeeded in the latter category.

I "went through college," as we used to say, and through a seminary designed to turn out conservative clergy. I attended graduate school and received an M.A. and Ph.D. in English and believed that I deserved to succeed in life.

For ten years I taught theology and literature at a well-ranked seminary as a tenured professor. Before that, I had served a congregation in Delaware and, for a while, as an editor and writer for a church agency.

Following a severe back injury, sustained while swinging a five-iron on a 150-yard hole in Delaware, I also became an alcoholic. I had not planned to become an alcoholic. Not once during my youth had I said to my parents, "When I grow up, I'm going to be an alcoholic."

After a disc rupture, however, an orthopedic doctor decided I needed barbiturates to force me to sleep. I was experiencing terrible pain in my lower back. To this day, I cannot adequately describe the agony of that time. To allay the pain, I took the pills and also drank beer or wine in what had always been for me a healthy social pattern.

I did not know whether I deserved my injury or not, and I didn't really care. I knew, however, that somehow I had to cope with the pain and keep on working. In a short while, however, I could no longer predict just how many beers or bottles of wine I would consume in a given setting. I became an alcoholic. That was a real mess, believe me.

Eventually I went through treatment for chemical dependency and nervous exhaustion, and I emerged as a healthy but somewhat crestfallen middle-aged man.

Unfortunately, after my treatment and recovery, I experienced vocational catastrophe. The board of directors of my seminary decided it wanted a new and more conservative faculty. In a move unprecedented in modern church history, the board fired most of its seminary staff on the grounds of insubordination and heresy. Along with 50 others, I lost both my job and my vocation virtually overnight.

For many years I had believed that I was a failure. I had pursued outward success in order to compensate for my deep feelings of inadequacy. Now my worst dreams seemed to have come true. Not only did I feel like a failure—I *was* one.

2 • Turning Point

After my seminary board had released me and my fellow faculty members, I went on to other jobs. Once again I became a pastor, and a nontenured lecturer in English at a college—this time in a beautiful Virginia town in the Blue Ridge Mountains. For a while I was also totally disabled with rage, self-pity, and a nagging backache.

Since I was a chemically dependent person, I could no longer escape my feelings by hiding in a bottle. The bottle had become suicide for me. And though I may have considered suicide unconsciously, I never did so consciously.

Outwardly, my life was really not that bad. I had a job, some good lifelong friends, and a great family. In spite of my failure and loss, I loved my family members more than anything else in the world, and I had other loves as well, including literature, tennis, and music.

And though I fretted endlessly about the loss of my teaching job, with all its status and vacations, I generally liked my church work. Most of the time I even believed in what I was doing. Yet at age 50 I continued to experience constant self-pity and resentment against God-knows-what.

One evening I decided I needed a little relief from my problems. I thought that I deserved a good drink. That was a big mistake. Slowly but surely thereafter, I began to lose control over alcohol. If I thought I had problems before, now I developed problems of crisis proportions.

Back in Treatment

Within six months I again lost control, not only over my alcohol consumption, but over every other aspect of my life. I let everyone down, especially my family and members of my congregation. I ended up in another treatment center—where I began to recover once again.

I wish I could say: "In the treatment center I met a therapist who said to me, 'Turn your life over to a power greater than yourself,' and I did that and was happy ever after." But that didn't happen. The ways of God with people are always more complicated than Hollywood would have us imagine.

While in treatment I was helped by a good counselor name Caroline. She was also a recovering alcoholic and was working for the recovery of other alcoholics. She invited me to turn my life over to a power greater than myself—to God as I understood him. I tried, but I ran into great complications.

Those who suffer from loss and failure must grasp one thing immediately: turning loss and failure over to God is not child's play. We do not carry out this process easily—certainly not by "going to church" or talking once or twice to a pastor.

I came out of treatment feeling merely "frizzled, stale, and small," but surely *ready* for recovery. I was ready to believe that God would and could help me. That was a big step for me. Therapies and therapists of the conventional type had accomplished little or nothing for me. I realized that God had to do something, or else the jig was up.

I discovered through treatment, however, that God could not produce the changes in me that I wanted until I approached God with total honesty. To put things another way: because my need for God was total, I could not *pretend* to believe or trust in God.

Throughout my life I had done much pretending about God. I began to realize then that I had lost my ability to accept and therefore to fully accept God already at the time of my brothers' deaths. My parents also seemed seriously affected by those events. Together we may have lost our capacity fully to understand and to accept both God and the world in which we lived. I had to accept these experiences of the past for what they were, no matter how painful they had been.

By saying this, I do not mean that my parents began to curse God or turn to lives of crime. On the surface, our family seemed exactly the same as always. We went to church regularly, though my father was now a church bureaucrat—indistinguishable from any other bureaucrat in any other business. He rarely spoke about his faith or ministry at all but only occasionally about problems of office management and personnel development.

As I remember those days, it seems to me that my mother also stopped speaking about this world in traditional religious terms. Perhaps she no longer saw God working around her. Christ did not seem to carry our burdens any longer. He did not function as a mediator between God and the world.

Already as a child, therefore, I began to sense that the world had lost its sacred quality. In the modern secular manner I began to allow things simply to happen, indeterminately and indiscriminately. I became prone to free-floating anxieties — resentments and fears over malignant powers, unnamed and unknown.

I remember that when I was in the fourth grade I discussed with a friend the question of who would go to heaven and who would go to hell. I remember both of us saying that we hoped we would go to heaven and be with God, our friends, and our relatives. We wanted to be "good" so that we wouldn't go to hell.

After the death of my brothers, such thoughts no longer came to me in precise forms. In my mind people no longer went exactly to heaven or to hell. People no longer existed in relationship with a God who could make such decisions. Though human actions still had vague moral weight, they no longer carried the moral consequences that would be given to them by a judging, forgiving, God. Without knowing it, I became gradually but thoroughly secular.

The first thing I had to do after treatment, then, was to go through the painful act of admitting to myself and to others that God did not always seem to exist in my world. That honest admission became a crucial step toward a new relationship with God. God began to work upon me in an entirely new way.

Honest to God

When I came home from treatment, I decided to concentrate on the honest relationship with God that had begun to develop in the hospital. In treatment I had tried to direct my prayers to God. Though I didn't find immediate relief, I was opening myself to God once again.

In our moments of deepest suffering we yet experience a desire to control or manipulate God according to our own desires and needs. And we cannot. But if we open ourselves to God—especially in our darkest hours—God will give us help, especially as we admit we are in and of ourselves quite helpless.

God, I believe, intends to give all good things to all people. God wants to give good things even to "bad" people—to failures and losers. To understand how and why God acts in our world, however, we must understand our present culture and move beyond mere positive thinking. We must discover the Christian gospel.

Before we begin that process, however, we must stop to look at our world. If we wish honestly to turn our lives over to God, we may have to give up many of our cherished secular ways of looking at our world. That is not easy. It certainly wasn't easy for me.

3 · Why Bad Things Will Always Happen to All People

In an attempt to answer some of the questions about God's will and presence in times of human suffering, Rabbi Harold S. Kushner has written a successful best-seller called *Why Bad Things Happen to Good People*. When I first read the book, however, I could not figure out why so many people recommended it almost as if it were the Bible itself, while I remained curiously dissatisfied with it. As I wrote this book, I came to realize why.

Kushner wrote about bad things, unforeseen and unfortunate events, that struck down good, law-abiding people. He wrote about terrible experiences that drive people afterward to ask, "Why me? What did I do to deserve all this? Why did God allow this to happen to me?" With honesty and insight Kushner tried to help good but grieving people adjust to serious losses.

I did benefit from his book and identified with

many of the bad things he described. I learned from him that I am not alone in my need to cope with severe losses in life. Above all, I found his book a welcome relief from the swarm of manuals on positive thinking created by writers and TV preachers. I was relieved to hear Rabbi Kushner confront the realities of illness, death, and other losses honestly and without pretense. Having experienced a terrible loss within his own family, Kushner could not pretend that such experiences are easily surmounted.

After I finished Kushner's book, however, I had a sinking feeling shared by other readers I have talked to. I discovered I was not exactly the "good people" he wrote for. I had the suspicion that I probably deserved my bad experiences as much as anyone else deserves such experiences in life.

Kushner, for instance, used the Old Testament figure of Job as a prototype of the good person to whom bad things happen. But I didn't feel like Job. In fact, I felt I had brought many of my bad experiences on myself by foolish decisions I had made years ago.

Job, you see, believed he was guiltless, deserving nothing but the best in life. He felt he had lived up to God's expectations perfectly. Because Job thought God treated him unjustly by allowing him to suffer, Job challenged God's right to treat him in this fashion.

But I simply didn't have the same feelings about God's rights. Because I believed I had done many wrong things in the past, I felt almost the opposite of Job—not insulted, but responsible for many of the bad things that had happened to me.

I realize now that I had had a New Testament rather than an Old Testament reaction to my sufferings in life. I had been greatly influenced by my faith in Christ. Though I had much to learn from my Jewish friends about suffering, I could not simply wipe away my Christian consciousness.

That knowledge left me in a quandary. Having read *Why Bad Things Happen to Good People*, I discovered as a Christian I had no pressing need to figure out why bad things had happened to me, a good person. Rather, I needed the faith and the forgiveness to surmount the bad things that happened to me, a run-of-the-mill and ornery person.

In the process, I discovered that the question "Why does God allow me to suffer?" seemed both presumptuous and archaic. Deep down inside I didn't ask that question, even when suffering severely. Furthermore, people counseling with me over failures and losses in their lives rarely asked the question either. Neither I nor my clients seemed inclined to figure out why bad things happened to us. We discovered, instead, that we had to find the power to get on with life.

Does God Even Exist?

Perplexity over God's role in human suffering arises out of a religious culture that is barely alive in our present world. Few of us today truly feel that God makes everything happen to us, moment by moment. We no longer sense a neat chain of cause and effect between God and our current illnesses, between God and the loss of a loved one or a job.

Many of us are not entirely sure that God exists—in our world or beyond—let alone whether God does anything to us or for us. We may wish we were more sure about God, especially when we experience severe loss in life. But we may find God's existence hardest to accept precisely during those times when we lose people or positions precious to us.

At the height of his sufferings, Job became angry at God; by contrast, many of us wonder whether God even exists. And as we question God's existence, we become rapidly confused over ourselves, our jobs, and all our important relationships.

Some psychologists tell us we become alienated toward the world we live in. We have considerable reason to become so in our secular culture. In the absence of God, we are forced under stress to rely on ourselves for survival, on the very ego that suffers confusion and depression.

Turning to Ourselves

Because we are not sure God exists, and no longer feel we live in a world preserved by a caring God, we must by default make ourselves into gods who can care for us. For obvious reasons we want to be "self-reliant." Whatever we do regularly, we feel we must do superlatively. In so doing we want to make ourselves feel like gods — independent, beyond all good and evil, vulnerable no longer to the slings and arrows of outrageous fortune. We learn to act as if society exercised no control over us—almost like a psychopath.

If we make self-reliance our goal, we will strive in our relationships not so much for mutually dependent love as for self-satisfying independence. We must feel that we are in charge. In the absence of a strengthening dependency on God, we realize that we cannot with feelings of self-esteem afford to rely on other human beings.

Because we know ourselves, we know that human beings are far too unpredictable to be dependable. We may try therefore to become comfortably self-reliant, even within our close relationships in our family or community.

"No more Mr. Nice Guy," we say to ourselves with self-congratulation, though in all probability we never were nice guys. We may worry not so much over the question "How shall I continue in life if I lose a loved one?" as "How shall I continue in life if I don't reduce my dependency on loved ones?"

When Self-Reliance Fails

Because we aspire to total independence, however, we tend to disintegrate emotionally whenever we lose something crucial for our self-image. In a secular society, self-reliant persons are not allowed to lose emotional control in any final sense of the word.

In fact, if we do fall apart when experiencing severe loss, plenty of people will inform us and others that we did not successfully "work out our grief," as if grief were a kind of mathematical problem subject to solution by means of the right formula.

Critical failures in our work or in family relationships may threaten our sense of self-esteem more completely than the loss of loved ones. The "law" in our society still tells us that losses are "acts of God." As the Germans might say, loss seems to be "thrown" at us; we don't have to feel responsible for such losses.

Since we feel morally responsible for our failures, however, we have great problems discounting and surmounting them. If we are fired from our job or divorced by our spouse, we cannot easily cultivate at the same time an inner sense of self-esteem and fulfillment. Because we become at that moment severely insecure and therefore dependent on others, we may lose our sense of advantage in our world, and therefore our self-identity.

When people previously believed God not only created the world but through Christ suffered with and for the world, they discovered that Baptism or initiation into Christ made suffering not only more bearable but intelligible. Even the slaves in our country could identify and exist in relationship with the suffering Christ, look forward to resurrection through him, and so bear up responsibly under terrible losses and deprivation.

As people in our culture have gradually lost faith in God the Father of our Lord Jesus Christ, however, and no longer live in Christ's sacrificial death and resurrection on behalf of all the world, they have also lost their ability to accept failure and loss from God. When they are in trouble, therefore, they do not know where to turn. No wonder they turn to the counselor—or therapist—who will, however, ironically fail every time he or she attempts to "treat" people who have also truly failed.

Now, since I have benefited from several therapists, I do not wish in any sense of the word to undermine or undervalue the place of therapy in our time. Above all, I cannot in the manner of some religious critics attack psychotherapists for their "humanism." In a humanistic culture we must, I believe, take our therapeutic enterprise with the utmost seriousness.

I shall, therefore, try very carefully to describe why I believe that any therapy rooted in a humanistic view of people will always fail those of us who need therapy the most. Since the majority of American therapists owe their vocation to the humanistic theories of Freud (and to some degree also to Thomas Jefferson!), we must briefly examine the therapeutic enterprise in this land.

4 • How Therapy Fails Us

The modern therapist has emerged as the person to help us make *our own way* in a cultureless world. In the absence of a cohesive society and therefore of a true religious establishment, therapists have become for us a type of priest. They act as mediators between our past and our present self and attempt to help us make peace within ourselves. In the process, therapists will usually assist us in surmounting our past, unless past experiences directly benefit us and contribute to our self-worth in the present.

Therapists, therefore, must, for the sake of our survival and "success," help us to be deliberately selfish and self-centered in the present. As a counselor myself, I can assure you that in the absence of a strong faith in God and in institutions sanctioned by God, many counselors may seem to have no other choice but to assist hurting persons to elevate themselves, usually by means of what the ancients called "false pride," to the point where they can feel good about themselves. In our society we choose to call false pride by another name: self-esteem.

In Search of Self-Esteem

Much of modern analysis and therapy revolves around the modern need to create a new and worthy self when an old self nurtured in traditional institutions disintegrates. When we don't know exactly who we are anymore, we don't ask Mom, Dad, or our pastor, "Who am I? What's it all about?" We ask a currently close friend with whom we can communicate our dissatisfaction with our upbringing. We search out therapists or support groups from whom we hope to gain power to escape from our past self, to form a new self in the present.

For that reason we hear a great deal in our society about our need to develop feelings of self-worth and esteem. In the absence of dependable supporting institutions and authority figures who will tell us what we're worth, we do not automatically feel that we're worth very much. And by ourselves we don't know what to do to feel better. As a result we become preoccupied with our feelings about ourselves.

We worry day by day in our secular society more over how we *feel* than over how we *think*. Because we cannot figure out intellectually what is going on in our cosmos, we fall back on feelings as the supremely important aspect of our being. Desperately we try to find someone who will tell us it's "OK" to feel all right about ourselves.

We look for someone, for instance, who will tell us we have no cause for "guilt feelings," by which we mean no cause for guilt itself over our past behavior, and therefore no reason for doubt about ourselves in the present. Therapists will try to help us overcome those doubts. Following Freud, the therapists of our society have rejected guilt as an "inappropriate" experience, which is their equivalent of "wrong." To call something *inappropriate* is as far as a therapist can go in damning something.

Most therapists, therefore, attempt to help us confront loss and failure as circumstances for which we have no final responsibility. They tell us we owe it to ourselves to overcome our sense of loss and failure by acting responsibly and congenially toward ourselves in the present.

Since in the modern metaphysic of therapy we never deserve to feel bad, we should be able, we are told, by self-serving actions to do away with bad feelings about ourselves—especially if we discover that our bad feelings stem from early childhood traumas created by parents and other authority figures over whom we had no control.

"What could be more simple, or more beneficial?" we may ask. If professional counselors and lay support groups gear us up to reject failure and guilt so that we might continue in our pursuit of success through self-cultivation, what on earth could be wrong with that? How could they fail?

I address the question with fear and trembling. As the sociologist Philip Rieff has said in his essay "The Impoverishment of Western Culture": "In a society with so many inducements to self-interest, 'self-realization' seems a noble and healthy end. The least valuable competitive position is to be self-defeating. The therapeutic cannot conceive of an action that is not self-serving, however it may be disguised or transformed." We criticize the therapeutic enterprise, therefore, only at our own peril.

Since our very life is at stake, however, we must

do precisely that, no matter how self-defeating we may sound on the surface.

Why Well-Meaning Therapists Fail

Modern therapy will always fail those in total emotional and spiritual need for two basic reasons we have already begun to describe.

First, in order to "free" us from our dependence on past authority figures and institutions, the therapist must invariably undermine precisely the authority once vested in these figures and institutions.

Second, our modern therapists must assist us to live and function as best we can by authority and energy we discover in self-centered pursuit of our own satisfaction. Both necessities pose severe problems for therapists and for clients who have experienced severe loss.

To the first problem. Since the common acceptance of the Freudian understanding of human nature, many people have assumed that each new generation must make a break with parents and similar institutions. But only in modern times (roughly since the 17th century) have people in the West felt the need to surmount their parents and the institutions of their elders in order to "find themselves"—and for a reason.

In modern times we have lost the basic security that family, church, and state may provide a child. We desperately search for self-identity in our pluralistic society because we lack the common security a cohesive community spontaneously supplies its children through strong institutions created by adults.

Thus, in each new generation we find our upbringing partially irrelevant or inapplicable in the society we currently occupy. As our society, under the impact of the communications revolution, changes more and more rapidly, the generations, in fact, grow shortter—perhaps as short as five years or so. Many of us, therefore, have to go through profound emotional adjustments many times in our early years before we finally determine, perhaps out of exhaustion and fear of old age, to hold fast to the person we presently claim as our self.

In our culture we may call this "growing up." Actually, we may tend in this process to grow *down*, regressing from levels of cultural development we may attain through our parents before puberty to new forms of childhood in the present.

Unfortunately, most of us probably have no choice but to regress. We may want the stability of the past but find that we cannot make that stability work for us in the present. We may wish we were like our parents, but discover we can't be. In a kind of desperation, therefore, we may break with the cultural stability we may have known. Though we may not like to admit it, we and our therapists pursue self-fulfillment always with a degree of desperation. Nothing in our life could be more difficult than attempting to overcome past authorities we took for granted in favor of the authority we presently call our self.

Starting All Over

If we must break with our past, we shall always to some degree start over with baby steps and find new ways to respond to present authorities, to peers and to events in our life today. In the process we either break to pieces or find a new way to survive by ourselves in the society we come only gradually to understand as we pit ourselves against it.

In the new society we learn that we must stand on

our own two feet and be self-reliant—which usually translates into plain *selfishness*. I, for instance, made a quick transition during my adolescent years from an ethic of Christ-like self-sacrifice to an ethic of self-fulfillment. I have not yet fully recovered from the shock of that transition.

In the process I lost both my emotional and my *vocational* bearings. For, when we choose by decision or by default to become self-centered, we lose our capacity for commitment to a cause or a calling we consider greater than ourselves. In theological language, we lose our capacity for *vocation*—from a Latin word meaning to "receive" a call, as it were from God. We then have to "find ourselves" and make our self a god.

The quest for self-identity, however, is quite literally beyond the capacity of any isolated self. When looking for our self, we always see, as in a two-way mirror, the disintegrated self we wish to replace. Without cultural sanction for our self, we cannot fully accept our self, let alone create a self we truly respect. We shall come to respect and accept ourselves only when powers higher than ourselves assure us that we are acceptable.

We discover that melancholy truth about life, especially when we lose something utterly important to us—or fail in something essential for our self-image. For when we fail our self utterly, we cannot then easily inflate our self in order to regain our power to exist. One might as easily inflate a punctured balloon from the inside out.

A punctured balloon must be repaired by outside power and force. No amount of wishful thinking or bombastic insistence on the powers of possibility thinking can ever repair a burst balloon or a burst ego.

A totally broken self cannot by itself find ultimate self-fulfillment—even through therapy. The broken person must find power for integration through other people and, finally, in a God who can put all broken beings together again.

When I was in great distress, for instance, I discovered that I could not healthily exist as an island divorced from community and the sanctions commonly accepted by a community. Without a community with which to identify, people like myself will simply flounder between psychopathic rejection of past authorities and moralities and depressive attempts to create authority and morality out of passing people and events in the present. No therapist could provide me that community.

Without commonly accepted values sanctioned by commonly accepted authorities such as God, however, a group of persons can never fully become a community. Communities emerge as people together accept common powers and values greater than themselves. No therapist can create those powers and values.

To explain more fully why I believe so strongly in communities of people who accept a power greater than themselves as a basis for existence, I want to continue my story. When I got out of the hospital, my real work with God in community began. Or, I should say, God began his real work with me to restore me to health and to help me accept my past, with others in the present, while looking forward without fear into the future.

5 • Waiting for God

While I was in the hospital, I prayed for two things: forgiveness and the power to overcome my feelings of defeat. I prayed mostly at night and felt as if I directed those prayers toward a corner of my room.

I did not direct those prayers at myself but rather outside of myself. Because I felt an acute need for God—as a dying man might experience need—I did not indulge in exercises in "personal growth" or in "ego reinforcement." I meditated—not in order to make myself feel better—but rather to open myself to God.

I rapidly discovered there was a huge difference between the two undertakings. When in the past I had practiced meditational exercises of the "trancendental" variety, I had attempted to relax or to build self-confidence by my own efforts. As I now prayed to God, however, I admitted that I could do *nothing by my own efforts.*

I discovered in the process that I did not aim my prayers upward toward any traditional God I had previously known in my childhood. When lying awake in my room at the hospital, I stared largely in the dark toward my window, watching the moon struggling to break through dark gray clouds.

Oddly enough, I thought little about the Christ, Jesus of Nazareth. My struggles with Christ were yet to come.

Significantly, too, I never once in treatment thought that my therapists were going to cure me. Because my counselor, Caroline, was herself a strong Christian and deeply committed to the Alcoholics Anonymous program of spiritual recovery, she made it impossible, I suspect, for me to think of her as my "rescuer."

I prayed to God. As I prayed, God always gave me some slight measure of relief and reassurance. God lifted my burdens ever so little each time. In the process I deposited a very small part of my will and life, for those moments, into God's hands.

I found it easiest to pray for forgiveness, and for two reasons. First, I felt genuinely guilty over my actions. I did not have guilt "feelings" but actual guilt for which I needed forgiveness from a Power more than human. Second, I could genuinely envision only God forgiving and accepting me. As the poet Heinrich Heine once said about God, not too flatteringly, "He will forgive. That's his business." I agreed with Heine, but in the most positive way possible. No one but God could accept me as I presently was.

As I prayed, I believed, at least for the moment, that God did forgive and accept me, no matter how others felt about me. To feel God's forgiveness, I did not have to locate God in society at large. God seemed simply there, in my room, sustaining me and shouldering a portion of my guilt for me.

Some therapists might tell me that I merely remembered my parents as forgiving people and transposed their attitudes, under stress, into God's attitude toward me. I find this idea interesting in an academic way, but irrelevant for my present needs.

Most psychological explanations for real feelings at crucial times of life are irrelevant at that moment. The reality of the feeling, not the "explanation" for it, is the critical issue for us when we experience terrible losses and failures in life.

No matter what the origins of our feelings about God's ability to forgive and accept us, most of us with some experience in life have the ability to ask God for forgiveness. We can pray for forgiveness because, deep down inside, we feel much more responsible for failures in our life than we like to admit in a culture sanitized against religious experience.

We should never try to eliminate guilt by pretending it does not—or should not—exist. When we do so, we jeopardize our relationship with a forgiving God. Rather, we should always try to turn our guilt over to God through prayer and confession, asking God to accept it and forgive it, as only God can.

Action Is Everything

To turn guilt over to God is to *do something* with God, an all-important step. To allow God to touch our lives, we must open ourselves to God. By contrast, most people who complain about God's absence or claim to be "atheistic" really make no effort to open themselves to God, even in the simplest ways.

In this way we establish a crucial first step for

spiritual growth—a step so obvious that we may think it unnecessary to state: in spirituality, *action* is everything. If we are spiritually inactive or cynical, we shall never exercise our spiritual muscles. Like an overweight jogger who gives up an exercise program in the first mile, we shall give up with the first effort. If we exercise for a while, however, we discover through practice that God begins ever so slowly to make us grow strong.

Next I found it necessary to pray for power greater than myself to change my way of life. Great losses and failures give us one advantage in our relationship with God. At times of failure and loss we find it very difficult to pretend that we are in charge of our lives and can change our lives by ourselves. Real losses and failures drive us to powers and people greater than ourselves—even if we believe for the moment that nothing can help us.

As I prayed for God's help in the hospital, I discovered that always at the moment of my praying God gave me relief from pressure. In the very act of turning my problems over to God, I believe that God began to convince me that I would not have to manage my life by myself. I would no longer have to resolve my problems all by myself nor through selfish actions somehow create my own feelings of self-esteem.

As I genuinely admitted to God that I could do nothing of myself to get better, God began slowly to make me well.

As I turned my life over to God, I discovered also that I could turn my life over into the hands of other people more advanced in spiritual understanding than I was. When I honestly admitted my needs to other people, I discovered that I could trust them.

They, in turn, began spontaneously to supply me direction for my own life.

The Art of Listening

I listened to them—no mean feat for me, since I am a talker. The ability to listen, I discovered, is an absolute necessity for spiritual growth. When we find people who both understand our needs and also feel they can help resolve those needs, we must listen to and learn from them.

Among people we truly respect and trust, we do not have to dominate conversation in order to build up our own ego. If we are down and out, we probably have nothing at the moment to contribute to the conversation anyhow. If we discover, under stress, that we still do the talking, we prove that we do not yet really believe we need help from God and others. When we stop trying to manage our own lives, we will begin listening to others. As we listen, God will also begin to give us the power to change.

I know of an elderly man who has for years been almost a professional God-seeker. He speaks at great lengths about his spiritual experiences of the past and about his needs for further growth. He loves to talk about his spiritual immaturity and calls himself a baby in the faith.

Around other people or groups, however, he rarely stops talking. He takes intellectual exception to almost everything said by anyone else and usually makes himself and others bitter in the process.

Predictably, he breaks off friendships and often quits groups, insisting that he gets nothing out of them—or that others are failing him. Until he stops talking and begins to listen to others, he will continue to destroy exactly those relationships through which God could begin to work on his problems.

If we are truly determined to find spiritual help from other people, we shall neither argue arrogantly with them nor break off relationships. When we need help we shall learn to share, rather than to compete, with others.

I learned that lesson the hard way—in the hospital. Through honest admission to others of my own defeats, I learned how God works quietly through others to grant us victory over our defeats.

God in Christ

When I got out of the hospital, I discovered that I had come to know God once again as the Father of my Lord, Jesus Christ. When I had turned to God, I had, willy-nilly, turned to God as I had once known him in the Christian church. Ultimately I was to recognize in Christ a person who had himself experienced terrible failures and losses and accepted people with similar experiences. I discovered God in Christ to be the only God available for failed people like me.

That discovery changed my entire viewpoint toward failure and loss and utterly altered forever, I think, my worries about "success."

In the next chapter I shall try to explain what happened to me and to many others who have had similar experiences with Christ. As we shall see, however, we have more difficulties recognizing the real Christ in our culture than we have finding a more abstract God. Some of us, in fact, may scarcely be aware any longer that the Christian churches claim that Jesus of Nazareth is also the "Son of the living God."

I have noticed, for instance, that many Christians,

when reading Rabbi Kushner's book about suffering, fail to notice that he predictably leaves Christ out of his picture altogether. He writes, after all, as a Jew.

If we leave Christ out of our lives, however, we leave everything out. Very shortly we shall see why.

6 · The Last God on Earth

God cannot be found within our culture at large. God can be found only in Christ and in the fellowship and sacraments of the church.

So I believe—no matter how curious those words may sound today. God, however, brought me to this conviction only through considerable efforts. In treatment I resisted the real Christian faith with every secular bone in my body. Furthermore, I discovered with frightening clarity that you and I have good reason for such resistance.

In the last chapter I recounted how I experienced God's presence while I prayed in my room. I also located God to some degree in the faithful affirmations of my counselor.

I found no God on TV. In general conversation, I heard nothing about God except such statements as, "Do you really think he exists?" Or, "Why did God allow this to happen to me?" Or, "Don't tell me you really found God in church among all those hypocrites!"

The patients intoned these words, I think, in order to claim their innocence of any responsibility for their lives. They were obviously concerned over why "bad" things had happened to such "good" people as themselves. Most of them, however, seemed unwilling to accept any moral responsibility for the bad experiences they had had in life. Quite simply, they were not ready to let God be God, especially if he were to pass judgment on their lives.

Furthermore, I read nothing about God in the newspapers and did not find him in the woods surrounding the hospital. Outside of my room and away from my counselor, I found little trace of God at all. God seemed not to exist in my cultural space of that moment.

If we wish to open ourselves to God, however, you and I do well to accept the general absence of God within our culture. We should not weary ourselves overly much by fighting that absence. No single person among us is capable of altering our presently secular society. Since our major media, our government, and our public educational systems are all profoundly "godless," we cannot render them sacred either by argument or by wishful thinking.

By that I do not mean that network announcers, or senators, or public school teachers actively eliminate God from the scene. In a capitalistic country we even say to ourselves that God supports our endeavors and gives some of our ceremonies, such as inaugurations, an aura of legality and finality.

In a secular culture, however, we try to prevent God from doing anything important. We relegate God to the status of the Queen of England. We allow God to preside occasionally over traditional rites of the realm, and thereby we are given the feeling that the culture has changed only very little. As a matter of fact, however, our secular society would function perfectly well—perhaps with greater ease—if God would disappear altogether from our common language.

God Still Lives

God can, however, still find us—even within a secular society—through Christ and through the church, which is, after all, Christ's body in the world. So long as God continues to live through the church, God never dies or disappears, even in a secular world. So long as God in Christ remains present in the Word and sacraments of the church, the church never becomes fully secular.

Because, however, we have become so accustomed to think and feel in secular terms—as if God had actually died—all of us have great difficulty conceiving of a God present in the concrete person and activity of Christ in his church. Even if we believe Christ to be divine, we shall probably avoid saying so lest we offend others who don't seem to feel that way. Thus, the person of Christ may become more embarrassing for us than the concept of God.

We may, for instance, prefer to think about God in very abstract terms—as abstractly as Rabbi Kushner does in his book *When Bad Things Happen to Good People.* Kushner tries with some success to absolve God from responsibility for our fate. The historical Christ seems, by contrast, very concrete, particular, and directly responsible for our fate.

Similarly, Bishop John Robinson, in his book *Honest to God*, wanted us to think of God as the "ground of being." When we call God "fate" or "ground of being," we make God seem less responsible for ourselves and also reduce our own feelings of responsibility toward him. In reducing responsibility all the way around, however, we tend to substitute intellectual abstractions for God's real presence in our world.

By contrast, the Christ of the one, holy, catholic, and apostolic church completely resists all efforts at abstraction. Either he is the living God, coming among human beings to heal them forever, as the Scriptures attest — or, as C. S. Lewis once wrote, "He's on the level of man who claims to be a poached egg." Either he is the resurrected Christ forever present through his Spirit at all times and in all cultures, or the church becomes lunatic in its affirmations of his person and accomplishments.

Theologians have long said that the church is stuck with the "scandal of Christ's particularity." Committed Christians claim that God entered this world in a particular person, Jesus, within a particular ethnic group, the Jews, at a particular time in history to rescue all who would respond to his coming. Through Christ's Spirit God is always present for us in our cultural space of the moment. Through that Christ, however, God places pressure on both our intellect and our emotions for a response to him now—a pressure that seems especially radical within a secular or conveniently "godless" society.

Some years ago I wrote in my book *No More for the Road* a chapter called, "Christ the Model." In that chapter I compared the sufferings and deterioration experienced by an active alcoholic with Christ's sufferings. I further compared an alcoholic's recovery with Christ's resurrection and expressed the idea that a recovering alcoholic, or anyone recovering from severe failure or loss, participates in the power and reality of Christ's resurrection. Through recovery, I wrote, a failed person gains faith to look forward to final victory over death itself through Christ's resurrection.

After reading the book, some persons praised the chapter as "religious," and others condemned it as "too religious." My chapter about Christ, therefore, became the *controversial* chapter of the book. For only in that chapter had I radically strayed from language and concepts commonly accepted by the general public. I had spoken of Christ in a way no longer accepted in our general culture.

The Disappearing Christ

How has Christ's disappearance affected our society?

Some years ago an alcoholic woman, Christian by background, came to me looking for help both for drinking problems and for anxiety reactions she experienced when she could not sleep.

I asked her if she could still pray to God for relief. She said, "Not really."

"I was raised a Christian," she said to me, "but no longer feel that Christ is present when I pray or when I take Communion. Sometimes I think God may still exist, but I don't think Christ is really God. So I don't pray any longer to God through Christ, the way I was taught."

By these words, the woman meant she no longer felt the divine and human Christ to be the mediator between God and the world, or between God and human beings. She was left, therefore, with a world where God seemed at best remote, at worst, absent. Without knowing it, she summed up a problem we all have with a god who is no longer "Christian."

When Christ seems to us to lose his role as the mediator between God and human beings, God becomes merely mysterious and remote—so far removed from us as to be either unthinkable or even unnecessary for our existence. God becomes something like fate.

As a merely historical figure, Christ continues to serve some purpose as an example for others. As a mere human being, however, he brings to our culture neither authority nor power sufficient to encourage people to follow his self-sacrificial way of life or to find relief through his death and resurrection. Our society has become profoundly secular due, in large part, to Christ's seeming disappearance from the scene.

A majority of Americans may continue to say in national polls that Christ is "divine." In fact, however, the majority of Americans reveal in their lives little evidence of faith in Christ's divinity, especially in his resurrection. We do not so much reject the divine Christ as simply ignore him.

The Last God on Earth

After hospital treatment, however, I discovered I could no longer afford that cultural luxury. As I tried to pray to God, I realized I needed once again to take Christ with utter seriousness—for Christ had become for me the last God on earth. Everything else was an intellectual abstraction for me.

Though I had tried very honestly and repeatedly in the past to accept Christ as the source of forgiveness and life for the world, I realized how I had always given up on Christ all too easily, *whenever I found myself offended by his historical particularity.*

I began to recognize in myself a classic problem case within the Christian world. Though I needed and wanted a God badly, I didn't really want to accept a God who offended my own intellectual dignity or the intellectual and emotional dignity of my peers.

How on earth, I thought, could I openly affirm a God who offended my entire world by identifying himself with Christ? How could I accept a God who just happened, I thought, to offend my best secular friend of the moment?

My best "secular" friend, then and now, told me repeatedly that he believed in a "Higher Power" and tried to turn his life over to it—to "H.P." as he called it. But he couldn't come to terms right now with a God who entered history at a particular time in a person with a particular name—who lived, died, and rose, and asked for a response to those actions.

I struggled over my friend's reactions for a while, but then discovered that I could not afford to make his problems my problems. I had to act for myself. Since I couldn't pray to "H.P.," I had to do what my emotions led me to do: pray to God through Christ—as I had done when I was a child.

Why did I once again stoop to pray in this way? Because I had no choice. I had to pray as the person I truly was, mind and emotions. Since I truly needed God's help, I could no longer afford the luxury of intellectual gamesmanship. No matter how God's actions in Christ seemed to offend my intellect or emotions, I needed precisely the God in Christ whom I had come to know, however poorly, in my youth to cope with my failures and losses.

When we need God badly enough, we will approach God on his terms. If we can't approach him on those terms, we simply don't need God badly enough.

Difficulties with Christ

I do not, of course, want to downplay the difficulties of accepting God's reality and actions in Christ Jesus or to make jokes about those difficulties. Every committed Christian knows how hard it is to accept a God who comes in the person of Christ into the real world.

St. Paul himself called the gospel of Christ's death and resurrection a "stumbling block" for Jewish people and "foolishness" for Gentile people. By those words he meant that God's presence in Christ, especially in death and resurrection, would offend all people who felt God either to be a living being, wholly other than human beings, or a spiritual force which human beings could understand only through great intellectual effort.

How much more convenient for us, most of the time, if God remained merely an idea or force to contemplate with intellectual dignity whenever we felt like it. How odd of God to reach down toward us, instead, in the form of a human being, requiring us to respond to that effort.

I had reached the point in my life, however, when I needed precisely that sort of God. I began, therefore, to pray again, ever so hesitantly, to God through Jesus Christ. No matter how odd I felt at first, and how childlike, I persisted. And as I turned my life to God in Christ, I discovered God accepted it and began to give me feelings of forgiveness and power through the person of Christ. Through Christ's sufferings and death, God began to relieve my own sufferings. And through Christ's resurrection God began to give me the power to renew my own life.

I began to live again as one who had risen from the dead. For the first time since I was a child, I began to *experience* myself as a little Christ—a person who had been forgiven by him and empowered to suffer, die, and rise with him in my present life.

When I began each day to see myself mirrored in the person of Christ, I began by his grace and power to recover from my failures.

In Christ we do not *escape* our failures, but rather *recover* from them by his grace and power. In Christ we discover a "failure" available only to failures. In all the world there is no one remotely like him.

He is the last God on earth.

7 · The God for Failures

In the previous section, I suggested that we Americans do not so much reject the divine Christ as simply ignore him. In our media, however, writers and directors may also choose to recreate a Christ for our culture. When creating so-called Christ figures, however, modern artists tend to shape them to match their personal tastes in morality and popular psychology. In a word, they secularize Christ to serve their own cultural biases.

Since I have a Ph.D. in English, with a modern literature concentration, I realize now I had been deeply affected by literary efforts to recreate a modern Christ. Before I could approach the real Christ, therefore, I had to overcome my fascination with the many metaphorical characterizations of Christ I had come to know in contemporary literature, and even in theology.

For example, in his story "The Man That Was," D.

H. Lawrence created a Christ figure who swooned on the cross, revived afterwards, and went forward to fulfillment in sexual union with a temple prostitute of the Egyptian goddess Isis. Lawrence translated Christ's resurrection into a genital *erection* and subsequent consummation in intercourse — an experience the sexually frustrated Lawrence believed to be fundamentally necessary for human self-realization and salvation.

In his novel *One Flew Over the Cuckoo's Nest*, Ken Kesey created an equally obvious Christ figure named McMurphy who developed in his fellow patients on a psychiatric ward feelings of self-esteem through lessons in bravado, alcohol, drugs, and, again, sexual intercourse. In a culture obsessed with the need for varieties of sexual experience, we might expect many of our artists to create a "Christ" able to satisfy our sexual fantasies of the moment.

Though McMurphy finally "gave up his life," as it were, by receiving at the hands of maniacal medical staff members a prefrontal lobotomy, he also gave to his friends the will to leave the institution and begin a life of unrestricted debauchery themselves.

What could be better? Don't large numbers of people in our culture want to believe with all their heart that the undisciplined and amoral life is also the totally fulfilling life? Kesey's "Christ," therefore, tends to sanction our quaintly wishful thinking about a "free" and untrammeled existence, where we grab all the gusto we can get without fear of consequences.

Kesey, Lawrence, and virtually every major writer of our century have created Christ figures to fit their own needs for personal approval and sanction within their culture. Christ has been made over into everything from a sexual pervert to a clown, from a drunken millionaire to a hobo hitchhiking on the road. And many of us readers have been intellectually stimulated by these efforts—as a detective might be stimulated by clues leading to the identity of his major suspect.

The Real Christ

If we truly wish help from God in Christ rather than mere aesthetic stimulation, we have to resist that modern urge to recreate Christ to satisfy our present notions of human need. If life is more than bread itself, it certainly comes to much more than forms of art.

When I left treatment the last time to return to my family and my congregation, I discovered I had to move far beyond the Christ figures I had enjoyed in modern literature. If I truly wanted help from God, I had to turn to the Christ of the historic church, and for a simple reason: there is no other real Christ.

Literary and film Christ figures are obviously products of human creativity and the need for aesthetic gratification. The Christ of the historic church offers, instead, judgment, forgiveness, and the promise of a renewed life that lasts forever. He offers us a way of recovery from failure and loss through suffering—through faith beyond failure.

In Christ, the last God on earth, we do not escape from our failures but receive forgiveness because of, and in spite of, our failures. In Christ we receive forgiveness from a person who himself experienced "failure" in this world and felt completely free to accept spectacularly failed people as his friends and followers.

If we read the Gospels of the New Testament carefully, we discover that God through Christ routinely attracted the "losers" of his society: prostitutes, thieves, traitors, and probably a good many bankrupt tradespeople. The successful business people, the political and religious leaders of this country ultimately decided they had to kill him—in part because he attracted a lot of riffraff who could, in their estimation, have become a dangerous political force threatening their established social security.

Jesus had not even one close follower with any social standing worth talking about. His immediate disciples, who through their witness to the death and resurrection of Christ would change the world, were by and large hand-to-mouth fishermen and farmers. Among the great apostles of the early church, only Paul could claim a good academic background and some professional training.

Even Paul, however, never made it into a profession. Before he converted to Christ, he frittered away his time arresting Christians for trial before the Jewish courts in Jerusalem. Paul was himself a failure forgiven by Christ and propelled thereby to make a witness to the gospel so powerful that not even the Roman Empire could hold it back.

The God for Failures

I was similarly attracted back to the Christ I had come to know in my youth because I saw in him a type of "failure" himself and therefore a source of relief for the failures I had experienced.

Because I believed Christ had experienced failures in life and death, I could also accept his forgiveness for my own failures. Because I came to believe once again that Christ was divine, I felt that God himself could forgive my failures and grant me power to move through faith beyond failure.

In our present psychological jargon, we call this

process *identification.* As strange as it sounds, I identified in the modern manner with Jesus of Nazareth, crucified and risen, and thereby opened myself to him in a way I had never fully done, even as a child.

I now believe that our own sufferings and losses become fully acceptable to us only as we believe that God suffers totally with us and for us in Christ. We can never—in Milton's words—"justify God's way to man." Neither Job nor Rabbi Kushner could figure out why bad things happen to seemingly good people. Both of these men of the Old Testament age acquiesced to God's will—or fate—and induced others simply to accept the divine mystery of it all.

In Christ, however, God does away with the mystery of his will. God makes his will infinitely clear and reveals himself as one who is ready to enter the human struggle on behalf of the human beings involved. Because God continues to love humanity and a world which has broken away, he chooses to suffer for us that we might finally share with him freedom from all suffering—even from death itself.

New Testament writers frequently describe God's sufferings in Christ with and over his creation. In his second letter to the Corinthians, St. Paul states that God made Christ to be "sin"—that is, made him to suffer as a sinful and condemned man—even though Christ never sinned. God allowed his Son, Jesus, to suffer so that we could be made right in our relationships with God. God finally accepted and justified us through the death and resurrection of Jesus Christ. Paul wrote, "God was reconciling the world to himself in Christ, not counting men's sins against them" (2 Cor. 5:19).

A suffering God will bring the entire suffering world to a glorious peace and fulfillment through the suffering but risen Christ. So Paul affirms in his letters to the Corinthians, the Romans, the Ephesians, and the Colossians. He surely must have been firmly convinced of God's good will for all people—and the entire cosmos. And so I came to believe in God's good will.

In Christ we see God bridging the gap between himself and a suffering humanity in a suffering world. In Christ's resurrection we see by faith God's ultimate will to heal all failed people through our own resurrection to perfect and peaceful life. God wills to heal us finally, no matter how we suffer and die in this life.

The Meaning of the Resurrection

The church stands upon this faith. Faith in the resurrection separates the Christian church from the religions of the world—even from the very best of them. For in the church we do not claim the ability to find God or unity with God. We claim God's will to find us, to forgive, heal, and finally restore us to life even after death.

Such belief can easily be challenged by nonbelieving people in a secular society. I have let myself be challenged too many times in my life to pretend otherwise. When, however, I accepted in faith the will of God in Christ to heal me of all my infirmities, now and forever, I experienced a feeling of health and wholeness I cannot describe in words.

After I returned from treatment the last time, I began to recover by that faith and hope in Christ. Every day I was conscious in a new way of sharing the sufferings of Christ with others and drawing on his healing power. Because I believed he suffered with me and for me, I felt no resentment toward God or others and no need to ask the question: Why me?

Since I knew Christ had suffered for all human beings, I might just as easily have asked the question: Why *not* me?

God in Christ guarantees you or me no immunity from failure, loss, and sorrow. Rather, he promises to accept and forgive us when we fail and experience loss. God promises to see us through the very worst kind of pain—emotional and physical—that we may experience in life.

As I gathered with supportive people after treatment, I grew stronger and stronger in that conviction, for as I was to learn over and over again, God works through the Word, the sacraments, *and his people*.

8 · God's Strength for Our Weakness

Within the first six months after my return to active church duties, I discovered some dozen alcoholics and drug addicts within my community—addicted people who would never have spoken to me about their problems unless they had come to know I had a similar problem.

Some were in Alcoholics Anonymous and kept a low profile. Others entered treatment and A.A. after counseling with me. Some remained active in their addictive behavior but in touch with me and our little group of alcoholics and other addicts within our area.

Similarly, persons with many other kinds of problems — family, marital, emotional, economic — began coming to my door. As we shared our common experiences in Christian terms, I discovered that I felt completely comfortable with these people. Because I felt comfortable, I think I enabled them to reveal their experiences of faithlessness and failure. I could then invite them into a relationship with Christ who suffered with them, forgave them, and offered them a life beyond failure, lasting forever.

With a growing sense of honesty, I found I could invite the people of the congregation — currently troubled or not—to receive Christ in the sacraments of the church, to find Christ in the Scriptures, and in the mutual gatherings and conversations of common people. Many of us together began to recover from our human condition and all its perils and pains through Christ.

Because we live in a secular society, I know I offer a way of gracious recovery through God which seems, in the poet Hopkins' words, "strange, spare, and original." The sacraments of the church may seem to aggressively secular people the quaintest—or silliest—practice of Christian people.

The church, however, must continue to offer Christ to needy people in concrete and practical ways through the sacraments, as well as through preaching, teaching, and fellowship. For in the sacraments of the church, people may obviously continue in faith to see God providing a bridge between himself and his world.

For that very reason, a person honestly and vitally concerned about opening up to God's power and grace should at least be willing to enter the community of that church where God is said to be literally present.

My Return to the Traditional Church

When I left treatment, I had no choice but to return to the nurturing church I had often chosen to ignore in the past. To function as a Christian after treatment, I found it necessary to seek sanctuary in the Christian church of historic tradition—in my case, the Lutheran church — which claimed the ancient creeds and the liturgical and sacramental tradition of the ages.

Within the great historic and traditional churches, which claim the entire history of the church as their history and all the saints as their saints, failed people will find Christ through words, sacraments, and above all through the affirmation of faithful people of the present.

Within the traditional and ecumenical churches, no one person can make a private interpretation of the Scripture or of church traditions and demand public acceptance for it. No one person can claim a private insight into the person, death, and resurrection of Jesus Christ as a foundation for his church, or for his TV ministry. No one can dismiss our Lord's suffering, sacrificial death, or resurrection without becoming a tiny, private voice in the wilderness outside the church. And no one may elaborate further than the creeds and classic denominational confessions upon the story of Christ or the history of the early church.

Within the traditional churches, we find the historic Christ affirmed in Scripture and regularly revealed in the lessons and sermons of the church. We hear God affirmed as creator and recreator of the church and, indeed, of the whole cosmos.

Within traditional churches we find the Holy Spirit affirmed as God present in our world and hearts, now and always. No matter how our culture may try to squeeze God out of his universe, the traditional churches will continue to place God firmly at the center of and beyond the universe—in Christ and his Spirit, and therefore in the center of and beyond human hearts.

Precisely the traditional Christ of the historic church became my basic resource for recovery from loss and failure. Through Christ I found myself, in the face of losses and failures, released from my need to justify God or myself. I discovered I could release my long-gone little brother into Christ's hands, worrying no longer over why he died, or over my own guilt accumulated over the years since his death.

Faith Restored

In Christ I came again to believe that all things work together for good to those who love him. I came slowly to believe that the sufferings of this present time are not worth comparing with the glory God shall finally reveal through us in Christ Jesus.

Ironically, I found faith and the favor of God in the church of my ancestors. I found there a tradition and community into which I could fit myself without violating my modern personality or identity. Not only could I let God be God in my life and daily turn my life into his hands—I could also let the church be the church for me, through Word and sacraments, prayer and people, in the world. I could look forward to a world to come through the resurrection of Jesus Christ.

In the jargon of the moment, I began to "grow"—through God as I came to understand him in Christ Jesus.

We can all experience that growth in our lives when we accept both the successes and failures of our lives, without resentment and without self-pity, through Christ. We can't live a *charmed* life; we can have a *forgiven* life in Christ.

When disaster strikes, we don't have to ask, *why* me? But rather, *how* may I accept in Christ responsibility for what has happened and move forward in hope, helping others? We can in Christ live as *God-fulfilled,* rather than merely as *self-fulfilled,* people.

We can turn our will and our lives over to the care of God as we understand him in Christ. In the next chapter, we discover how this works—for all kinds of people.

9 • What Do You Deserve in Life?

I know a man who sputters inwardly and outwardly day after day because he feels most people are against him. He also has a bad shoulder and tears muscles while playing touch football. Actually, I think he is too frail to play football, but he does so because he feels he *deserves* to play.

Now a man who pulls a muscle every few months certainly seems to have something to complain about. He has every right to become testy, hasn't he? My acquaintance is a perpetually angry man. People in Alcoholics Anonymous would say that he constantly sits on the "pitypot" saying, "I don't deserve this, I do not!"

In resentment, he yells at his wife, berates his children, and breaks off relationships with well-meaning people. Because he always holds others responsible for his problems, he destroys friendships as fast as he makes them.

When drinking and complaining to his friends, my acquaintance will say, "I can't even have good sex in this condition." The final blow. His injuries thwart his "rights" to sex, he thinks, and therefore seems to remove from his grasp his basic and inalienable right to the pursuit of happiness itself.

My acquaintance, of course, confuses happiness with his ability to gratify his most immediate desires. He is intensely "modern"—a baby in adult form. As you might expect, he is fiercely competitive and unable to accept the slightest threat to his person.

By contrast, I once had a client, a lawyer, who when jogging one morning was hit in the back by a runaway U-Haul truck. My former client is now a paraplegic. He is also a faithful, often happy, father, husband, and good friend to many. His close friends call him Ironsides.

After his injury, he did not get perpetually angry, yell at his family members, or decide God didn't exist —the unkindliest cut of all. He did not break off all his friendships to gratify his anger. He didn't even have to participate in wheelchair marathon races to prove himself a man. He has told me he has no need any longer to prove that he can finish races—on foot or in his wheelchair. He daily accepts his present state in this world.

As you might guess, my former client is a traditionally Christian person who believes he is fortunate in God's gracious scheme of things to have a life, family, friends, and the chance to work at what he calls his "vocation." He feels he deserves no more than that from God.

He also identifies strongly with the suffering Christ and feels that God allows him continuing life in order to show love to people close to him. By means of his legal skills, he helps many people he calls "needy."

Though he gives much, he feels he deserves nothing more than God in his grace gives him. He is reasonably happy in Christ.

What you feel you deserve in life largely determines your ability to feel happy or unhappy in life. And you will feel you deserve in life what you think life—or God—*owes you*.

Job, for instance, had many unnecessary problems with his losses because he thought God owed him the large family, the camels, sheep, and donkeys which he lost.

In fact, God owed Job and me nothing. We deserve, I believe, nothing at all from God except judgment for our wrongs. Anything good we receive from God we receive graciously as a gift. To believe so is to release ourselves from a great deal of miserable self-pity and resentment. Had I really known God's grace as a child, I think I would have been far less self-pitying and resentful as an adult.

If you think the world, or God, owes you what Thomas Jefferson quaintly called "life, liberty, and the pursuit of happiness," you will have big problems in life—especially as you grow older. You may have peak moments of self-inflated well-being but no lasting happiness or peace of mind at all.

The pursuit of happiness requires health, leisure time, and money. Most of us have little of the above and therefore can't even pursue what we may think in a secular age are our inalienable rights.

If we believe, however, that God, creator and re-creator of his world, owes us nothing but chooses graciously to give us his gifts of life and other luxuries, we shall find ourselves much more at ease in our world—no matter what we possess, and no matter what we have attained.

My Right to Status

Most of my life I secretly felt that I deserved status —recognition bordering on adoration—and a comfortable margin of money. I pursued status more than money, recognition more than happiness itself—and when I thought God existed, assumed he owed me such status.

Deep down inside, I probably believed that recognition as a "star" professor and maybe a writer would bring me happiness. I coveted my professorship, therefore, not so much because I enjoyed teaching or the fierce competition with my academic colleagues but because of the status other people granted me in my position.

I loved having student "disciples." I loved making speeches before common people who assumed, because I was professor, that I fathomed the very mysteries of the universe.

Now both my wife and I knew that people in our society routinely overrate professors of humanities. Nevertheless, I enjoyed the position and, after losing it, missed all the status and the free time the position allowed me. I was very much like a majority of the professional class in a secular society — insulated against reality by the reasonably successful pursuit of my goals.

I learned the hard way that current success and comfort is no guarantee for continuing success and comfort. I learned the hard way that to demand and expect gratification is finally to ensure unhappiness and lack of gratification. To demand and expect status and recognition from others is finally to lose it.

Miserable old people, for instance, are invariably people who have demanded self-gratification for a lifetime. When they lose even their physical ability to feel comfortable in life, they turn into perpetually resentful and self-pitying persons.

Comfortable and loving older people have usually demanded little for an entire lifetime. Now that they have in their old age very little—even little health—they still feel fairly treated and at ease with their lives.

Giving Up Our Self-Demands

We shall experience true freedom and ease in this life only when we give up our self-centered demands for all the goals we think will bring us happiness. We shall finally achieve and *retain* none of the selfish goals we currently pursue. That is a law of our existence. We can be happy only when we live day by day, accepting what we have from God as gifts of of grace.

I sometimes wish life were otherwise. I have, however, discovered that Mother Nature guarantees us nothing and finally gives us the same. God alone gives graciously over and beyond that which life and death brings us in nature. As we turn our lives over to God (as we understand him), we are released from the demand to fulfill ourselves, and we begin to experience life—in whatever form we have it—as a gift from God. When we fail, or lose people or things dear to us, we still experience God's forgiveness and power as means to help us through the suffering and pain to peace again.

My friend in the wheelchair has experienced precisely that peace.

If we can take a further step and identify with the Christ who suffers, we shall even in our worst moments never feel completely alone or forsaken. Even in our worst moments we shall anticipate peace and well-being once again through God who endured suffering and death with us and conquered them through Christ.

With practice we come to know that God has seen us through rough times before and will see us through them again. We shall recognize that God himself, in ways we cannot fathom, has been through the rough times also and continues to experience those times with us.

Such is the nature of God. God loves us and cannot help but stand with us and for us in our sufferings. God calls us, therefore, to draw on his power day by day through spiritual exercise and discipline.

For most of us, however, no discipline is easy—especially no spiritual discipline. We shall see why.

10 · Spiritual Exercise

To turn our lives over to God we must develop by his power a daily pattern of spiritual exercise. Without a spiritual discipline, we shall invariably revert back to self-management and the demand for self-gratification. I learned of my need for such exercise after my last experience in treatment.

I discovered, as a newly aware Christian person, that I could experience peace and freedom in my life only insofar as I daily — many times a day — turned my life over to God as I understood him.

Fortunately, I had made a mess of my life once again and no longer wished to manage my life by myself. I wanted God as my manager, my source of forgiveness and continuing peace of mind. To satisfy my wants, however, I had quite simply to pray to God —not only in church or within a support group—but by myself day by day.

I began each day with prayer, with meditation, and readings in devotional materials of my choice. I did so, and do so, deliberately and doggedly. When I don't feel like praying or reading, I force myself to do so. For the discipline of prayer and meditation comes no more easily than the discipline of jogging or mowing the lawn. I must keep at it.

When I fail to turn my life over to God at the beginning of the day, I invariably try to manage the day for my selfish purposes and thereby bring unhappiness both to myself and to others. In my demands for success and self-gratification, I also breathlessly botch up my work. When I know, however, that God has my life for the day, I always have a relatively good day with others. And because I worry less about succeeding, I actually accomplish more.

Whenever I find myself preoccupied with worries about success, I deliberately stop what I'm doing and remind myself that I have no rights to success and therefore no reason to worry about success. Whatever it means to me and others, success rests in God's hands, not mine. If I am successful in my undertakings, I receive that success undeservedly, by God's grace in Christ.

During the day, I must frequently remind myself that God has my life and will and that I shall go along with him for the day. Again and again I must remind myself that I deserve nothing more than he chooses to give.

Though I may choose to work hard and responsibly during the day, I recognize that no one owes me a reward or even congratulations. And though I may pray for health and well-being for the day, I believe that God, who suffers for me and with me in a suffering world, owes me no immunity from bad experiences. Many people around me have very bad experiences each day. In the sort of world I live in, I know I may be next.

During the day I frequently say and pray the Serenity Prayer, and I recommend it to everyone: "God grant me the serenity to accept the things I cannot change, courage to change the things I can, and the wisdom to know the difference."

In this prayer we accept our human inability to manage our lives, but we recognize also our power, through courageous and responsible actions, to change some circumstances and some aspects of our behavior during our lifetime. Above all, we pray humbly for the wisdom to recognize the difference between things we can, and things we cannot, change by ourselves.

To recognize that difference is to experience maturity in our living.

Live and Let Live

In my experience we can, with great courage and humility, modify our behavior. If we humbly recognize our tendency toward anger, resentment, and self-pity, we can modify our outbursts of anger and resentment toward others.

We cannot, however, substantially change the behavior of other adults through criticism or manipulation. If we truly wish to bring about change in others, we can do so only by changing ourselves.

To remain relatively happy in a relationship with God as we understand him, we simply have to give up our self-demands to change other people. As people regularly say in Alcoholics Anonymous: "Live and let live." By criticism, judgments, or manipulation, we cannot change a single person, except to make him or her angry at us.

To live happily in God, we must turn not only *our* lives into his hands, but we must turn the lives of *others* into his hands as well.

An extraordinary number of people make themselves and others miserable by trying to shape up others for their own benefit. They may spend a lifetime writhing in resentment and self-pity and never recognize the source of their own problems in themselves.

Many outwardly successful people make themselves miserable by imagining that others choose through their behavior to make them unhappy. A woman once spent over an hour describing to me how her college-age daughter had "destroyed" her life by dropping out of college. "From the time she started high school," she said, "she did everything possible to make me mad. I had to take her out of high school and put her in a private school," she said, "and still she wouldn't change. Now she sits up in her room all by herself, and it serves her right," she told me.

When she finished, I felt as if my head were spinning. What seemed so obvious to me seemed to have escaped her completely. In her demands to create a daughter to fit her needs, she had destroyed the very possibility of a relationship with a daughter. Her present isolation and loneliness struck her as a due reward for her *daughter's* poor behavior, not her own. The daughter had made her unhappy, she thought, and thus got what she deserved. Her daughter, however, had *not* made her unhappy. She had accomplished that feat on her own.

No one, you see, possesses the power to make you unhappy, though you may allow others to do so.

Avoid Resentful People

If you wish to experience peace and happiness beyond all loss and failure, beware of friends and acquaintances who always complain about their lives and criticize other people and groups. Beware of people who tell you how others have let them down, hurt them, or failed to satisfy their needs. If you give them a chance, these people will drag you down to their own level of self-destructive pity.

Self-pitying people (often they call themselves "sensitive") do not so much want your friendship as they want corroboration of their judgments against others. In all probability they have little capacity for love and friendship. They are unfortunate but classic examples of misery loving miserable company for its own sake.

If you can, maintain a safe distance from resentful people. When you turn your life over to God each day and pray the Serenity Prayer, you will have no need to share in the resentments of others, nor add yours to theirs. Spend your day, if possible, among peaceful and accepting people who live and let live, as Christ would have us live.

Our Lord finally judged only judgmental people. He always forgave those who stopped judging all others except themselves. And to all people Christ said, "Judge not, and you will not be judged." You will finally not be judged and discarded by God—if in faith you can refrain during your lifetime from judging and discarding others.

At the end of the day I strongly suggest that you once again turn your life and will over to God as you understand and rapidly analyze your behavior for the day. In A.A., people call this process "doing a moral inventory." I call it *confession.* Turn your failures, mistakes, and losses over to God and ask for forgiveness and acceptance—through Christ. Try to believe that God, who knew failure in Christ, forgives your failures and at the end of the day accepts you as you are. After praying for the power to change yourself in the future, compose yourself for sleep.

When you get into such habits of prayer and meditation on a daily basis, you will find it difficult to demand more than you truly deserve from God. As you demand less from him—or from life—you will find yourself more easily and more frequently satisfied and happy with your life.

Friends in Need Are Friends Indeed

I have an alcoholic friend—a very close friend—who happens also to be diabetic. When younger, he lost a leg to the disease of diabetes. He has also had a heart attack and has experienced crushing losses within his family. Not long ago he developed an eye problem that blinded him in the left eye. For weeks he went about fearful and depressed over the possibility of permanent blindness. During that time, however, he managed almost on an hourly basis to do one thing: to turn his life over to his God, his Higher Power, as he likes to call God. And in doing, he remained sober and managed to function responsibly at work and in his important relationships.

I consider his feat a minor miracle. So does he, though he would not say so. For, through God as he understands him, he has learned to live humbly and to accept what he gets in life. He insists that at one time in his life he was one of the most arrogant and destructive men alive. I take his word for it.

Now he seems to me to be one of the most humble and constructive men I've ever known.

I need my friend very much and talk with him several times a week. I need nonresentful people who have deep insight into their own capacities for destructive self-pity. I learn constantly from such people how to continue my spiritual life within a secular world.

If we wish to continue and develop a spiritual life outside of the settings where spiritual life thrives, we must seek out people who practice a spiritual life.

Development of a spiritual discipline does not come by magic. It comes by good association. The world offers us, through media, most professional therapists, and educators, nothing for spiritual growth; yet many people have discovered through failures and loss the need for such growth. When we stick close to them, we shall grow also.

On *Entertainment Tonight,* a program dedicated to "star worship," I heard a rock star say one night: "If you don't grab what you want, you will get what you deserve." His friends in the group then hooted and hollered in appreciation of his hateful remark. The man seethed with resentment even on the air and spoke only to get what he thought he deserved—recognition from others who were similarly resentful.

When you have no need to grab from others, you will be satisfied with what you get from others, and from God, as you understand him.

Even when suffering from severe losses of loved ones, or of health, or from failures in your work or your relationships, you will be able to continue in relative ease by turning your life—such as it is—into God's hands. Many people have learned to do so. I shall tell you of a few I know.

11 · Living with Loss

About a year ago, a friend of mine from the Midwest called me at my office. I was quite surprised to hear from him and thought he must have something important on his mind. He did.

He told me that earlier in the week his son had died in a car crash on icy roads. He had just attended his son's funeral. Now, he simply wanted to share both the news and his grief with me.

"I was sitting here all by myself in my office," he told me, "and felt myself becoming a little faint. I just wanted to talk to someone."

We talked. And though I do not recall the conversation all that well, I do remember that we shared experiences with losses in our lives. We talked together about reactions we had had to the death of persons close to us. And we shared our common faith —almost wordlessly—that God through Christ sees us through all sufferings and pain to health and well being again.

I felt strangely uplifted by my friend's willingness to share his experience with me. He honored me with his decision and spurred me on to follow his example in sharing my own losses with others.

We know today that we should not "hold grief in" but share it with others. To hold grief in is to ask for continuing anger, resentment, and self-pity later on, we are told. To hold grief in directly after an experience of loss is to project that grief in bitter and hostile reactions against others later on. We hear less, however, about how we can do it, how we can share grief at the time we experience it. It's much easier to talk about than to do.

We will discover within ourselves a capacity to share real grief to the degree we believe also in God's capacity to help us surmount our grief. We will share real grief over losses of loved ones—or of other things dear to us—most easily when we have faith in a God who shares our grief and carries us beyond all failures and losses. I know from bitter experiences with carefully concealed anger and grief over the deaths of both my brothers how hard this can be.

Because at that time I could turn to no real God to bear my griefs, I have most of my life kept my sorrows to myself and taken them out on others. Since I didn't trust God with my pain, I didn't trust other people with it either. I became too frightened to share much of anything going on in my life.

Most people who refuse to share grief are both frightened and embarrassed over their feelings. They know deep down inside they can't handle them or accept them. And they are afraid others will criticize them for these feelings. As a result, they bury them and pretend to others that they are too "strong" to be seriously affected by them. Often, they bury themselves also in some form of work, of play, or in a hobby, over and beyond their normal responsibilities.

Though we must, after experiencing serious losses, try to get back to our normal work as quickly as possible, we should never overload to cover our feelings of loss. If after the loss of a loved one we suddenly become workaholics, we are probably burying our true grief in our work. We begin to turn ourselves into "driven" persons.

I have known persons who, when seriously injured or ill, insist upon "getting to the office" immediately or participating in social activities which add to their problem rather than relieve it—all because they don't want to admit to themselves or others that they have lost anything through illness. I've known several people who, against medical advice, checked themselves out of hospitals after injuries or operations, because they could not think of themselves as disabled persons.

I once spent two weeks on a beach with a cast on my foot—perfectly miserable—because I refused to admit that a broken bone in my foot bothered me in any way whatsoever. Even with a ton of sand in my cast, I pretended to my family and friends that life was just a bowl of cherries.

Many of us will do remarkably stupid things in order to avoid sharing our real feelings over losses with others. Through fear and faithlessness, we make ourselves miserable.

If, however, we believe that God can and will through Christ carry our griefs and bear our sorrows, we shall — almost without thinking — find ourselves sharing that grief with others who believe in the same way. We won't worry about what others think of us. If we're truly grief-stricken, why on earth should we worry whether people think we're strong or weak?

Strong and loving persons always feel grief and show it. Weak and selfish persons tend to feel and show less grief and worry much more about the reactions of others to them.

Self-centered people constantly imagine that the whole world around them watches their behavior and congratulates them for every sign of strength they show. Unfortunately for self-centered people, their acquaintances see in them more selfishness than strength and regularly tell each other about it. In the process, the selfish person becomes more and more isolated and less able to develop the faith which allows both for love of others and for self-acceptance.

Faith and Love

Faith-filled persons are usually loving persons. Love requires the risk of faith in others. Faithful people, therefore, tend also to feel grief deeply. Since they believe God loves them deeply, they learn also to love others as deeply as they believe God loves them. If they are Christians, they learn through Christ to give themselves in love for others. As a result, they also feel the loss of others very deeply.

The Gospels tell us Christ cried two times. Once, he cried before the grave of his recently deceased friend, Lazarus. A second time, he cried over all the inhabitants of the city of Jerusalem. He foresaw, I think, the Roman armies destroying that city shortly after his death. And since he was a loving man, he grieved in advance over the fate of his countrymen.

When I was in the hospital, I also cried in front of a number of other people, something I've never done before or after. I mourned what seemed to me at the time the total loss of my very self.

I am frank to say I have never grieved over anybody else so strongly. I discovered that mourning the death and loss of a loved one is relatively easy compared with trying to mourn the loss of your self.

At the time, I felt terribly weak. I believed I proved my weakness through my tears. Only later, when sharing that experience with friends and family members, did I realize how God provided me grace and *strength* in my moments of honest grief over real losses of honor and good name. For in truly grieving, I also believe I opened my heart to God's healing and forgiving Spirit and allowed God to bring about changes in my life.

Since that experience, I try to share my experience of grief and loss as quickly as I can with my family members and my closest friends. I share with those who have themselves a faith in a higher power—a God, hopefully Christ—who enables us to overcome all trials and sufferings, even death itself. I share through prayer with God in Christ, who I believe suffers with me and for me.

It takes faith to share grief. It takes faith both in God and in other people to share our losses. If you lack the faith to share with others, I strongly urge you to attempt through daily prayer and meditation to acquire at least a measure of faith. Try as best you can to share some of your real feelings with those whom you trust the most. If you belong to a congregation which worships regularly, join in the worship and the sacraments of that church and share yourself with the people of that church.

Time may heal all wounds. I believe, however, that time, plus God and other people, brings healing about wholesomely and finally.

I have known all too many people who nourished wounds and losses for a lifetime, all because they could and would not, when the losses occurred, share them with God and with others. In self-pity and resentment, they kept their losses to themselves. They refused to give them away to anyone else.

I know of two older women who some years ago lost children very dear to them. One lost a daughter in a freak automobile accident. Her daughter was riding with a friend who somehow lost control of his car, left the road, and overturned in a little creek. The occupants of the car all drowned.

When the mother heard the news, she was visibly stunned. When I first tried to talk with her, she could not speak back, but seemed almost deaf and dumb. She merely cried silently and gripped my hand and the hands of others who in love for her came to comfort her.

Her family and friends, I suspect, made no attempt to explain to her why the accident had happened or why God had allowed it to take place. No one tried to explain why this bad thing happened to her, a good person. They all simply assured her that God in Christ —the way she understood God—would comfort her and sustain her even through this experience. I heard one of her older friends say: "You will teach us all how to live with suffering."

One week later this remarkable woman came to worship with her fellow members in her congregation. She asked for and heard her pastor pray for her and her daughter. She talked calmly with others, and assured them that God was still with her. Everything was going to be all right, she said.

And we were all relieved through her relief. We were not only happy to see her recovering from her own pain and sorrow but strengthened by her recovery. She helped us overcome fears over terrible losses we might also sustain.

Every person who recovers in faith from loss assures someone else that they also can recover in faith from loss. Faith is infectious. In our own sufferings we depend upon the faith of others far more than we shall ever know in this world.

The second woman lost a son in a similarly freak accident. He was returning from work one evening during winter. Somehow he managed to turn onto a one-way street going the wrong way. The gathering darkness and a light snowfall confused him, we think, and allowed him to run head-on into an approaching car. He was instantly killed.

When I first visited the woman, she seemed very calm and self-assured. She told me and others that she could handle the situation. Since she was divorced, she went by herself to the funeral home to purchase a casket and personally made preparations for the funeral services. She refused any substantial help from friends or even from family members.

When I told her I sympathized with her in her grief, she informed me that she could "not afford grief at this time." She had "too much to do."

Since that time, this woman has withdrawn from her friends, has quit her job and taken another one, and has dropped out of her congregation. Though she appears to have aged considerably, she always insists she's feeling fine.

She seems, however, to have changed overnight from an optimistic, outgoing, and compassionate person to a bitter and resentful one. Nothing pleases her any longer. She finds fault with her closest friends and feels that all the groups she once supported have failed her. Therapists would say that she projects her resentment over the son's death on other people.

When we can't share our grief and our resentments over our losses with God and with others, we will take out that resentment on innocent and unsuspecting people. And because they cannot understand our resentment, they will naturally reject us in turn and thereby increase our own resentment.

Resentment always hinders spiritual growth. As Bill Wilson, cofounder of Alcoholics Anonymous wrote, "Resentment is the chief offender" in life. It almost killed me—but now I know why and how.

12 · Why Resentment Is the Chief Offender

When I returned from treatment the last time, I experienced an almost overwhelming temptation to lash out in resentment at people critical of my behavior. I felt I had to resign my job immediately, not only because I knew I had failed in my work, but also because I wanted to retaliate against those whom I felt had judged me critically, without even comprehending the nature of my illness and loss.

Fortunately, good friends and compassionate members of my congregation refused to accept my resignation. They urged me to think it over and to talk it over with others for a while. Some months later, I realized that I had acted both in guilt and anger against people largely supportive of me. If they did not understand the nature of my illness, most of them continued to care for me anyhow.

Had I simply quit in anger and guilt, I would have been stuck with those feelings for the rest of my life.

I would have taken out my resentment not only on other people but on God himself, I think, and would have continued in the behavior pattern I developed as an adolescent.

As an adolescent, I think I began taking out my revenge upon God for my misfortunes. In the modern manner, I stopped "believing" in him. Like Ivan in Dostoyevski's *The Brothers Karamazov*, I felt that the suffering of even one innocent child made God unacceptable. I refused to give God a chance. At the time I never learned whether he would help me accept the suffering of my brothers or of myself. As a consequence, I failed to comprehend for much of my life *God's* continuing sufferings through Christ for all of his creation and his power to help us in *our* sufferings.

Had I failed this last time to turn my losses and grief over to God and to share these feelings with others, I suppose I would have closed my mind against God altogether. In depressive resentment, I would have discovered the intellectual reason most people finally reject God: they find him unjust. As I grew even older I would have gathered all sorts of intellectual reasons for finally disposing of God from my life. And I would have wasted my time and my life in the effort.

When we experience severe losses in our lives, the last thing we need to do is to explain them to ourselves, to intellectualize or rationalize them away. Though the question, "Why has this happened to me?" will come to our minds, we shall simply make ourselves feel worse by trying to answer it.

When years ago I lost my professorship, I tried for a long time to explain this event to myself. I felt as innocent as a Jewish victim of the Nazi Holocaust. Yet I could not figure out why God had allowed such seemingly hateful people to deprive me and my family not only of my profession, but my home and my entire fellowship of friends. Sometimes, in my depressed and agnostic moods, I decided that "fate" had done me in. At other times, I tried to convince myself that God would somehow "use" this miserable experience for my own good, for the good of my church and my world. I existed, it seemed, in constant conflict within myself.

I realize now that I was simply awash in feelings I could not handle on my own. I would have done far better to have talked them out with friends and counselors rather than try to figure them out in my own mind.

I believe now that God allowed these events to happen. I think also that very frightened people made these events happen. I wish to leave the matter at that. Thinking about it resentfully makes me suffer all the more. Continuing in my new work in relationship with others, however, makes the suffering gradually diminish and helps me to believe that in God's good order all things work together for good for those who love him and place their trust in him.

When God Allows Bad Things to Happen

When we recognize that God *allows*, without *causing*, bad events to occur in our lives, we make considerable progress in our functioning relationship with our healing God. Rabbi Kushner comments on this distinction: God doesn't want to make you sick; God doesn't want to make you suffer, he says. "He didn't make you have this problem, and he doesn't want you to go on having it, but he can't make it go away. That is something too hard even for God.

. . . God helps us be brave . . . and he reassures us that we don't have to face our fears and pains alone."

Though I am not sure what Kushner means when he says, "that is something too hard even for God," I can offer my own interpretation. I think God, when creating human beings, gave us freedom to accept his relief in suffering or to reject it. We may open ourselves in faith to God or close our hearts against him. I think God also created an entire world capable of suffering. Why we and the whole world suffer, I am not certain—though humans contribute much to that suffering. From personal experience, I know only that God can relieve our sufferings when we turn to him in faith.

God can't force us, however, to turn to him or to anyone else for help when we suffer. That is "too hard even for God." Or I would prefer to say: because of the way God created us free, he makes it impossible for himself to force us to faith—and to the healing he provides to us when we trust in him.

Certainly, I believe with Rabbi Kushner that we don't, when suffering, "have to face our fears and pains alone." Because of the healing ministry of Christ, and because of his resurrection, I believe that God does not even will to make you or me sick or make our loved ones die. In a suffering world where evil and death routinely occur, God allows—as it were—the unthinkable to happen. God allows us and his entire living creation to die.

In Christ, however, God promises us resurrection to final life through faith. Through the Word and the sacraments of his church, God gives us a foretaste of that resurrection by his presence in the suffering world. And God promises finally to create new heavens and new earth in which his love and healing spirit will prevail.

Paul says that the whole world is "groaning as in the pains of childbirth" for reasons he does not fathom—while waiting for the culmination of God's plan of healing for his world. The Christian poet Gerard Manley Hopkins called our world "bent." He also said "the Holy Ghost broods" over it "with warm breast and ah! bright wings." The Christian writer C. S. Lewis also called our world bent—out of shape as it were—suffering from evils which Christians have always traced to the fall of humanity from a state of perfect faith in God, the Creator of the world.

Personally, I cannot fully fathom what troubles our world. I do believe that Christ suffered in this world and for this world. I know that while he was in this world he healed the sick and the dying. I believe he rose from the dead and promises life beyond all suffering and death in his resurrection. I believe that the Holy Spirit does brood—as over an egg—over this bent world and will give birth to a new world free of pain and suffering. Above all, I believe God has frequently given me a foretaste of that new world to come through release from pain and suffering already in this world.

I know, however, that God guarantees me *no freedom from sufferings to come.* I know that I will soon die and pray for the faith to accept that death. Even more strongly, I pray for forgiveness and for the power of other people to help me in the hour of my death. I will need lots of help.

How Bad It Is

Though I appreciate Kushner's statement that "when we reach the limits of our own strength and courage, something unexpected happens," and at those moments we discover "God is on our side," I can't, from personal experience, believe that the unexpectedly good *always* happens, or that we always and automatically *discover* that God is on our side. In my romantic moments in the past, I have wished such statements were true. In my worst moments of loss and failure, however, I have not always found that the serendipitous event occurs. When grieving, I have not always been, in C. S. Lewis' phrase, "surprised by joy."

Upon the death of his wife, Lewis himself went into deep depression, from which he barely escaped when he stopped looking for a reason why or for some unexpected good turn of events and simply turned his life over into the gracious hands of God.

The world is much worse than Kushner allows. The world is sufficiently rough to make most popular positive-thinking manuals on the market thoroughly ridiculous. Many of us have already been wiped out spiritually and emotionally beyond the ability of any therapist, clergyman, or self-help writer to describe. And when we have been truly wiped out, we could only cry out for help. We could merely pray for faith that God would raise us from this death—from a death of spirit which simply prevented us from going on by ourselves at all.

In those moments, many of us have in total helplessness simply turned our lives and wills over to the care of God as we understood him. Nothing more, but nothing less. And because we came to believe in God rather than to explain him or his actions, God indeed saw us through death to life. He allowed us, in fact, to become proof of his power.

Years ago I visited a good friend and member of my congregation in the hospital. He had suffered a serious heart attack that day and, though conscious, did not know whether he would make it through the night. He was in that vital 24-hour period people experience after a heart attack. If they live through those hours, their chances for recovery skyrocket. During the period, however, they live literally on the edge between life and death.

After I had prayed with my friend and reminded him of Christ's death for his sins and his resurrection for his life, he thanked me and said: "If I am 'translated' tonight, make it a moment of celebration for the congregation."

As long as I live, I shall never forget those words. He meant: if I go to my God in death tonight, help the congregation take joy in the resurrection of us all.

That's the way I hope and pray to approach my own death: in faith and in concern for others who also need faith.

How Good It Is

In faith, I believe I can finally confront and surmount all losses—no matter how staggering they are for a time. I hope I do not speak glibly. If I were to lose my wife or any of my children, I have no idea how I would respond. If I were to receive the news today—which is quite possible—that I shall soon die, I have no idea how I would respond. I hope and pray that I might respond with the faith that carries us beyond all losses.

When I fail in the future, I hope I will have the same faith.

I reserve the problem of confrontation with failure to last because I believe in failure we confront the greatest obstacle in life. In failure, we may develop even the need to die by our own hand. Because of failures, we may develop the need to inflict further losses on ourselves and others rather than sustain them.

There is no public honor in failure. Since it is, in our culture, unthinkable, few people ever write about failure. Unthinkable or not, we all experience it all the time. Only those who are truly arrogant and filled with false pride imagine themselves immune from failure. Those who are truly arrogant can skip the next chapter.

The rest, I hope, will read on.

13 · Living with Failure

A patient in treatment for alcoholism once said to me, "The doctor tells me I may have a brain tumor. Say a prayer for me."

Deeply moved, I told the patient, "I'll pray every day that you get a negative diagnosis."

"Negative!" said the patient. "I *want* a brain tumor. I'll take anything over alcoholism."

The man thought he wanted a tumor rather than an addiction. He felt he could live with a terrible, and perhaps terminal, diagnosis for which he had no moral responsibility more easily than he could live with alcoholism—which at that time seemed to him a totally unacceptable failure.

Down through the years, many patients in treatment for addictive disorders have not only prayed for physical illness but tried for years to pretend to themselves they were physically sick with everything except addiction. Family members, and perhaps even the doctor and employers of the alcoholic, may have pretended he was sick with anything except alcoholism. Alcoholism seems a failure too great to accept.

In their attitudes about weakness and failure alcoholics are no different from other people in our culture. People will accept the most horrible circumstances of fate—or, if you want, of God's will—more easily than they can admit and accept the realities of personal failure.

In our culture we are driven to resist admission of failure tooth and nail. People who pursue fame and fortune at all cost cannot fail—or so the media and many therapists tells us. To fail in pursuit of success is the modern equivalent of damnation.

When asked about the possibility of military failure in the 1982 expedition in the Falkland Islands, Prime Minister Margaret Thatcher quoted Queen Victoria, who reputedly said, "Failure is not a word in my vocabulary."

Failure may not be a word in your or my vocabulary. We may have convinced ourselves that a combination of hard work and true grit will ward off all failures in our lives. But if we think so, we are tragically mistaken. If nothing else, we have rejected the commonsense experiences of our youth.

Born to Fail

Failure is, in fact, a routine experience in the lives of us all. We all fail and must learn to cope with failure. If we do not, at an early age, learn responsibly to accept our failures as real experiences, to turn them over to God and to other people, we will grow up spiritual and emotional cripples. We will develop the worst failure possible: *false pride*. For a lifetime we will imagine ourselves to be perfect when we are in fact perfectly flawed.

Psychological theory suggests the common experience of failure as one of the most basic elements in our maturation.

We are born with a feeling of built-in success and a need to fulfill all our desires. We demand from our parents every possible gratification. We want food and cry out for it. We want our diapers changed and cry out for change. We want liquids, particularly our mother's milk, and cry out for it, often in the middle of the night. We want to touch our mother and want her to carry us, and we cry out for her. Unconsciously, we imagine ourselves perfect and demand gratification accordingly.

Children are not born perfect. Children simply don't comprehend how selfish and demanding they are.

As children grow older, however, their parents help them understand that they are not perfect and do not deserve everything they demand. They learn that their demands are often selfish, excessive, and cruel.

Soon we human beings discover that a wail does not always bring a meal and a mother's touch. A cry or an angry slap at mother does not make her pick us up. We discover, instead, that our weeping and wailing land us behind closed doors in our bedroom, or worse.

The older we get, the more we discover how selfish we are and how much we have to modify our selfish behavior. We discover that our demands for success do not meet with favor from everyone around us. In the company of brothers and sisters, we are not rewarded for bopping our sister over the head with our fist and taking away her toys. Instead, mom bops us and gives sister's toys back to her.

When we go to school, we discover that all our schoolmates demand as much from us and the world as we demand from them. And either we fight it out with our peers, withdraw in defeat, or learn by experience to share with them.

To learn to share, however, we must experience one moral failure after another and accept defeat responsibly. As others refuse our own selfish demands on their time and person, we learn that we are not the center of the universe, or even close. We learn so *by failing*. We fail to get exactly what we want, and thus learn what it means to live in the human fellowship.

Forgetting How to Fail

As we grow older and move into high school, we may forget the lessons we learned through failure. We may lose the humility which allowed us to join the human race. In our culture, we may find ourselves driven to revert—or regress—to the level of a little child.

While denying the possibility of failure in our pursuit of success, we may become an overgrown adolescent. We may, in fact, develop a personality disorder, the most common, perhaps, of all modern disorders: narcissism with symptoms of paranoia.

That's a complicated way of saying we may decide we're number one in our universe and imagine everyone else is out to dislodge us. A great many "adults" in our culture today are nothing more than overgrown adolescents still playing king of the hill. As many women play queen of the hill as men play king of the hill.

I believe our modern obsession over becoming king and queen of the hill is a peculiarly secular one. Since we have no God to rule over our lives, we must make ourselves ruler over whatever domain we conceive to be our own. Because we cannot admit and give over our failures to God, we must deny them to ourselves and others and bulldoze ahead to maintain as long as we can the illusions of success.

In previous Christian cultures, by contrast, most people accepted the reality of daily failures in life and confessed them accordingly. "Sane" people never pretended to be perfect. Everyone felt themselves deserving of God's judgment and even condemnation. No one pretended that the greatest achievement in life was to be a personal success at anything.

The great achievement in life was variously called by Christian people the "vision of God," "salvation," realization of God as "gracious," or the acceptance of God as ruler of heart and world.

Without a God for whom to live in our secular culture, we face an almost irresistible urge to deify ourselves. And to deify ourselves, we must reject as best we can failures and the feeling of failure in our lives. We say: "I need a sense of self-esteem, not failure. I need perfection, not repentance." Many pop psychologists, from Dr. Joyce Brothers through Jane Fonda, tell us we need self-esteem beyond everything else. We must not think a negative thought about ourselves. We can do no wrong. To force ourselves into such a frame of mind, however, we must lie endlessly about ourselves and the realities of our lives.

Escaping the Trap of Self-Glorification

To get out of this self-destructive trap—to live with failures—we must develop the capacity to admit to failures. By now, I hope you realize I am not saying anything obvious or easy to digest. Most of us in our secular culture will make ourselves miserable for a lifetime because we have no capacity to admit to ourselves, to God, and to other people that we have ever failed in anything.

What can we do to begin to admit failures to ourselves, to God, and to others?

If we wish to begin living realistically and honestly with our failures, we can decide to sit down during the next few months and reflect quietly upon the failures we know we have experienced in our lives. If we can write, we can put those failures down on paper.

We can begin with our earliest memories of our life. When we have completed our descriptions of failures, we will probably be astonished at the sheer number of them, but also deeply relieved as we get them on paper and out of our system.

If we can then share what we have written with God and another human being (or beings), we will begin to live peacefully with the realities of past failures. We will also begin to develop the capacity to share honestly our failures, when they happen, with God and other people.

To share our failures with others who understand failure is to find relief and forgiveness. To share with God is to receive through Christ forgiveness for failure and renewed power to continue life by his grace and power, rather than by our own. To share failures with others is to accept others when they also fail.

Twice in my life I have written down my failures of life on paper and shared them with God and with another human being. Almost every night of my life I try to share my failures with my God, as I understand him in Christ, and pray for forgiveness for those failures. As I try to pray, I receive forgiveness and power to continue the next day.

If we write out and share our failures, we must be rigidly thorough and honest with ourself. We dare hold nothing back. When we know in years past we injured our brothers or sisters, good friends, or employers, through selfish and cruel actions, we should write about it. When we remember how we cheated and stole from our parents and lied to them, we should write it all down.

We dare not pretend that our parents are responsible, somehow, for the miseries and failures we presently experience in life. If we pretend so, we shall never be able to accept responsibility for our life in the present.

In the Twelve Step Program of Alcoholics Anonymous we are asked to write an "inventory" of our lives and share it with another person. Frequently an alcoholic decides he should share with a pastor, especially an alcoholic one.

The Universality of Failure

I have heard the most incredible failure stories you could imagine—stories you would not believe if you saw them in your newspapers. I have listened as men or women described how they killed others in car accidents, in barroom brawls, in "domestic" fights, while in drunken stupor. I have heard parents describe how they drunkenly drowned their children in bathtubs and let them fall out of apartment windows.

One woman told me how in a rage she one day set her cat on fire and incinerated her. The cat had missed her litter box and messed up the floor. Goodbye cat.

I have heard men and women describe some of the most startling sexual misadventures known in the annals of psychologists, clergy, or novelists. I have heard decent, law-abiding, rich, and sophisticated women of society tell of trysts with deranged and drunken sexual partners in squalid surroundings that defy description. I thought I'd heard the stories to end all stories.

Yet such moral failures are commonplace in the history of humanity. We know little of them because we keep the story of our own failures to ourselves and drive others to do the same.

As my best alcoholic friend says, "There are eight million stories in the naked city, and seven and one-half million of them are mine."

What are the most significant and universal failures we experience in our society? Failure in work and failure in marriage. All around us people fail in their work at school, or on jobs, and in marriage. And yet we cannot share these common failures even with family members and friends.

The reason is plain. If we find ourselves failing on the job, plenty of plain people all around us, and authors and therapists, tell us we can't fail — or shouldn't. "Dream the impossible dream," they tell us. "You can get what you want by hard work and relentless self-centered behavior."

Like a stockbroker, you can become rich if you get up at 5:00 A.M. and check with your London office. You can be successful, if you go back to your own office at midnight. You too can be like John Wayne and J. Paul Getty combined. You too can throw passes, like Terry Bradshaw, even when bald and toothless. You too can snatch victory from the jaws of defeat like Frank Sinatra, Kris Kristofferson, and Kenny Stabler.

By contrast, the author John Irving wrote three novels before he completed the *World According to Garp*. The first three books were "critical successes" but not market successes—which is a polite way of saying an English professor wrote nice things about them in the *New York Times Book Review* section, but nobody bought them.

With *Garp*, however, Irving had a popular success. Now he has been able to give up his teaching job and devote himself strictly to writing and TV appearances. However, as Irving recently said on the *Good Morning, America* show, "An author always feels he begins anew with every new book he writes." Success is fleeting.

I like Irving's honesty. He seems to know he has no guarantee of success in life. Life guarantees us nothing but ultimate failure in death. Yet most of us expend enormous energies denying the obvious.

I have known men in their 40s and 50s to go into deep depression because they didn't quite make the position they expected in the executive world of their company.

A friend of mine with a major company told of a colleague who went into a total funk upon hearing that he had been passed up for further advancement. For days on end the man locked himself in his office and wouldn't allow anyone to see him or talk to him.

Finally, one day my friend got a passkey from the maintenance department and opened the man's office to talk to him. At first, he didn't see him. Frantically he ran to the window, thinking he might have jumped to his death. As he ran past the desk, he saw two feet sticking out. Looking under the desk, he found the man sitting with his knees drawn under his chin. He was sucking his thumb. That day he entered a hospital for treatment.

After months of hospitalization, the man returned to his job and office, apparently able to accept his lot in life more comfortably. Or so everyone thought. On his second week on the job, however, he jumped from his office window—to his death.

He could not accept his failure to advance to the top. He chose death rather than to live with failure in his work.

We do not "allow" failure in our culture. Without help we shall continue in our culture to deny again and again the realities of our failures, until we die.

Free to Fail

What a great relief, therefore, to discover from the gospel of the Christian church that failure is forgivable by God in Jesus Christ. What a blessed relief to know and to come to believe that failures are inevitable but surmountable in Christ.

Failures will come. If we haven't failed yesterday at some significant test, or in some significant conversation, we will do so today. We may expect failure, but expect also forgiveness in Christ. We can prepare peacefully to turn our life over to God who knows all about us—all about our failures—and will forgive us and even empower us to try to do better tomorrow in the community of other failed people.

What a great relief it was for me to find groups of people in the world who not only accept failures as commonplace, but expect them. What a relief to find people who encourage us to speak of our failures, to share them with the group, and to discover that others fail also.

I could not have existed another day after entering treatment if I had not been surrounded by people who encouraged me to speak freely of real moral failures committed during my relapse, to speak freely of wrongs and of making amends to others. The day I began honestly to share my failures with others became the first day of a new life for me.

Failure need not be the end of the world for you, but rather the beginning of a new way of life. If we share failure with God and others, and accept forgiveness, we may begin again every day.

In Christ we discover that admission of failure is just that—the beginning of a new life in his forgiveness. Christ accepts finally all those repentantly conscious of their failure. We qualify for God's love in Christ when we fail and accept that failure humbly as reality. In Christ, and through people who consciously or unconsciously have received power and grace through him, you may receive faith to surmount failure—faith to live gratefully beyond all failure.

Many alcoholics in A.A. routinely say, I am a grateful alcoholic, by which they mean: Had I not failed miserably during my drinking, I would never have become honest with myself over my failures, never learned to turn my life over to God, as I understand him, and never grown into a morally mature person and a friend of other failures.

The late Karl Menninger, in his book *The Vital Balance*, said that some persons, sick with depression, emerge after treatment "weller than well." They have a peace and serenity they could not have acquired had they not suffered as they had. Having come through their ordeal and having honestly recognized their limitations and the limitations of others, they are ready for serene life within the human race.

I invite you — failures all — to life under God in Christ within the human race, that you might also experience faith beyond failure, and become weller than well.

14 · Faith beyond Failure

Robert Schuller, TV star, senior pastor of the Crystal Cathedral in California, and author of many books on positive thinking, has just published a startling new book called *Self-Esteem: The New Reformation.*

Schuller foresees a time when church historians will determine the "Church Age," or relatively good age of the church, to have existed from A.D. 100-1000. Then followed what Schuller calls "The Great Schism and Dark Ages," 1000-1516. Next came "The Reactionary Age," 1517-1999 (1517 being the year Luther nailed the 95 theses to the cathedral door in Wittenberg). In A.D. 2000, Schuller says, we will enter an "Age of Mission," an era of positive preaching about human potential and the need for self-esteem.

In the new age, Schuller says, we will "dream daring dreams and make private personal decisions; pursue risk (i.e., practice faith); succeed and be self-affirmed; fail and become a wiser and more self-reliant person; prosper and accumulate an estate (small or large); invest in human service-oriented enterprises; become financially independent from social, civil or corporate control and enjoy true economic liberation."

Unfortunately for now, Schuller laments, "Christians abound who are walking cases of uptight, defensive, angry, fearful, neurotic meanies. Why is this? What else can we expect if the call to conversion is a blatant appeal to a person's depraved, unworthy, totally sinful nature!"

"How then do we convert and change people?" Schuller asks. By calling them to esteem themselves, Schuller replies. Look to the stage play *The Man of La Mancha* in which the grand idealist, Don Quixote, meets a harlot named Aldoza, Schuller tells us. Like Jesus, Quixote, a glorious dreamer of the impossible dream, "despised and rejected of men," accepts Aldoza even though she calls herself a "kitchen slut." He thereby changes her into "Lady Dulcinea"! "The conversion was complete!" Schuller says. "She was born again!" She regained her self-esteem.

"I contend," writes Schuller, "and plead for a full-orbed theological system beginning with and based on a solid central core of religious truth—the dignity of man." Schuller then supplies a diagram of his "full-orbed theological system," offering a center circle called "A Theology of Self-Esteem," creating satellite circles called "A Theology of Communications," "A Theology of Social Ethics," "A Theology of Economics," and so on.

Schuller has obviously spent a good deal of time orbiting Hollywood. His theology of self-esteem and economic and social well-being also sounds curiously reminiscent of Thomas A. Harris' psychology of self-esteem and world utopia presented in *I'm OK—You're OK.*

Schuller, of course, will have success with his new book. For in America we experience a relentless need for assurances from self-proclaimed and successful prophets of emerging human "dignity." Desperately, we want to "become financially independent from social, civil or corporate control and enjoy true economic liberation." A yearning for such independence is part of our psychological heritage in America.

Our American Dream of Success

Our forebears in New England hoped to establish an economic and theological "New Eden" on American shores. Though they failed, their descendants have never lost the urge to do likewise, with or without theology. From Ben Franklin through Ralph Waldo Emerson, Mary Baker Eddy, Dale Carnegie, Norman Vincent Peale, to Robert H. Schuller, a stream of positive thinkers have urged us on in search of the utopia which eluded our more limited forefathers and mothers.

We Americans want and need to believe that we can change not only the world, but our own hearts, through rhetorical assurances of our basic goodness and chances for success. We will accept even a "full-orbed theological system" if it promises us success, self-reliance, and feelings of pride (currently called *self-esteem*). And any writer who promises us an estate (large or small) is bound to become our hero, and sell a lot of books as well.

Europeans dream fewer impossible dreams and buy fewer books on positive thinking. With longer memories and more experiences with national failures and losses, Europeans feel less compelled to sustain their egos through dreams of spectacular successes. Perhaps when we Americans have adjusted within the next decades to a stationary, or depressed, economy in an overpopulated world, we will also accept the realities of human experiences more easily with fewer demands for success.

In the meantime, however, people such as Schuller, Sylvester Stallone, and Joyce Brothers will continue to delude us with dreams I suspect they do not have themselves. Though these people have become successful by feeding on our pathetic, and even neurotic, needs for fame and fortune, surely they know what they have done. They have packaged in print or film an image of successful life currently demanded by millions of American people. And by creating that *possibility* of success, they have both sustained and magnified the American *demand* for success.

Surely they know, too, that the vast majority of people they address cannot possibly achieve the success they have experienced.

There will be no full-orbed theology revolving around human self-esteem. The year 2000 will not usher in some golden age of human virtue and social liberation.

The Real World

Look around yourself in the real world. Do you sense that you and other human beings, through a rhetoric of self-worth, will change the world in 16 years? Do you sense that you and other human beings will finally produce the glorious utopia our forerunners failed to create on American shores? Has the 20th century seemed to you the prelude to a Golden Age?

Though Schuller is half-right in declaring that

Christian people in the past have capitalized on pessimistic pictures of human nature ("the smelly swamps of self-shame") in order to "convert" people to Christ, he is simply wrong in blaming the Middle Ages or Luther and other Protestant "reactionaries" for creating a pessimistic picture of human nature.

In the past, people, Christian and otherwise, have painted gloomy pictures of human nature and dignity because they saw themselves and other human beings consistently doing gloomy things to themselves and to each other. And no current counselor or prophet of self-esteem can alter through therapy or rhetoric the gloomy realities of our human potential for evil—for failure and loss. In fact, by telling unsuspecting people they are basically good and capable of changing themselves and the whole world into a paradise, they guarantee their public a great and depressive letdown when paradise fails to materialize.

Delusion can never be a long-term substitute for reality. Delusion always becomes a form of mental "illness" or imbalance. Delusion about human nature invariably creates catastrophic effects both on individuals and upon society.

If Christians have in the past reveled altogether too freely in self-righteously satisfying condemnation of human "depravity," we people today, Christian or otherwise, will not undo the damage by pretending that human beings have all along been perfectly OK—though confused by "feelings" of guilt.

Exaggerated conceptions of worthlessness obviously will breed unnecessary fear, repression, and ultimately despair. Exaggerated conceptions of human worth, however, breed unjustifiable expectations of human nature and leave the door open for "life without guilt"—unrestrained self-gratification, psychopathic forms of behavior, and ultimately despair.

Neither extreme satisfies the needs of real human beings. Flawed as we are, we human beings retain the capacity to turn our lives in faith into God's hand, to learn from him how to accept and love each other. Since we are flawed, however, we will experience, even in a life of faith and love, many failures and devastating losses for which we are at least in part responsible and from which we cannot recover without God's forgiving and healing power.

As a failed but surviving human being, I believe that I receive such forgiveness and power from God as I understand him through the person of Jesus Christ.

Christ the Realist

For me, however, Christ is not a "grand idealist," pretending I am worth more than I really am—pretending, for instance, that I am a good person to whom bad things occasionally happen. For me Christ is rather a forgiving realist who accepts me in spite of what I am, and in spite of the evils for which I am responsible.

Christ accepts and enables me in a way that a Don Quixote could never do. Quixote, after all, celebrated the grand gesture of *noblesse oblige* in a time when the nobility and their gestures had disappeared. Quixote was a quaint but certifiable lunatic, yearning for a golden age which never existed.

Many of our current pop therapists, preachers, writers, and filmmakers seem similarly quaint but also certifiable. Like Ulysses' sirens, they beckon us on toward rocky shores with promises of success and of a paradisal community where knights rescue fallen ladies in distress and raise them by "grace" to noble stature. Unfortunately, knighthood is no longer in flower, and the gesture of *noblesse oblige*—even when offered by a superstar of our society such as Schuller—is nothing more than a gesture.

By contrast, the new age of Christ has not disappeared, nor can it ever disappear, no matter what the changes in our culture. Christ has risen from the dead. With him God has begun the recreation of our entire world. And through Christ God truly forgives us and thereby accepts us permanently and in reality. His forgiveness will produce within us real change—precisely at that moment when we turn our lives over in faith to him.

God in Christ truly can change Aldoza into Lady Dulcinea, but only when Aldoza realistically and responsibly turns over her past failures and losses through faith into God's hands.

The Powers of Faith

Faith makes all the difference.

When I experienced painful losses and failures as a child, I had not learned to turn my life over to God as I presently understand him. As a result, I learned instead the art of self-pity and resentment toward the world I occupied. Deep down inside I rejected God and determined that I must do my best to survive on my own in a wretchedly unpredictable world.

With a cynicism popularized as a "life-style" in our present culture, I chose long ago to look out solely for myself.

And though later in life I seriously and frequently tried to find through the Christian church and tradition the resources for living peacefully and sacrificially in my world, I never gave up my basic cynicism and pessimism toward my world. I never gave into my God as a higher power and therefore was unable truly to trust or love people around me.

Because I had lost my faith in myself and the world I occupied, however, I also found myself unable to respond with pious platitudes about positive thinking and self-esteem. And though I know many people today continue to respond affirmatively to a whole parade of positive thinkers cluttering the marketplace with their books, I remain simply amazed at their responses.

Failed people like me need fewer methods for self-improvement and more beliefs in a power who will finally save us from our failures at self-improvement. We need affirmation of faith in a God who will sustain us even when we fail to achieve the currently great American goal of success, self-esteem, and economic liberation.

I wish to know how to turn my life—both the good and the bad of it—over to a power greater than myself. I know dozens of people in my small town who similarly yearn for simple assurances of forgiveness for their failures and acceptance from God—and from people who know failure is not only possible but inevitable in life.

Though many of these people will search through self-help manuals to provide themselves a temporary fix, an instant illusion of power for self-improvement, most will finish the day knowing full well they don't have the power in and of themselves to make improvements.

I know large numbers of people in my town who yearn for relief and comfort in the face of terrible losses of loved ones and more recently of jobs vital for both their economic and emotional well-being. They yearn for a power to cope with their losses but do not find that power simply in themselves.

These people need no assurances and rhetorical promises from self-inflated prophets of prosperity. They need comfort from a God who shares their sufferings and cares about them. They want to know that God cares for them rather than why God or fate allows bad things to happen in their lives. They require help from people who have suffered as they have but have found a power greater than themselves which allows them to live on lovingly and productively.

All of us who have lost and failed often require God as we understand him in the person of Christ Jesus.

God Alive and Well in Christ

Though our society has greatly reduced Christ in stature and placed him on the shelf with other legendary religious heroes, we failed people need him now more than ever. Though academicians and journalists may systematically catalog Christ along with Moses, Mohammed, and the Buddha as the "great religious founders" of the past, we need him in the present.

We may find him alive and well in the worship and sacraments of the traditional churches and in many disguises in many groups of supportive people drawing upon a higher power they call God and secretly recognize as Christ Jesus.

I believe God sent himself in the person of Christ to suffer and to fail by the social standards of his day and so to reach out to failures and losers of every generation since.

Through faith in the resurrected Christ, all failures and losers may become winners and successes. Though I can't look to the year 2000 as the beginning of the age of self-esteem and human brotherhood and sisterhood, I do look forward to a new age to come, God's age when self-esteem and unity will prevail insistently and pervasively in the forgiving Christ.

In the meantime, you and I can accept our failures and share them with God and other caring persons. And in the accepting and the sharing, we will receive from God the power to live on day by day in relative ease and comfort.

We don't have to reach for the stars or believe the sky's the limit to feel at ease. Why reach for the stars when we can reach for the flowers in the ground each day, and from them make a bouquet?

I once gave my wife a poster which reads: "Happiness is the art of making a bouquet of those flowers within reach." She has the poster on her closet door in our bedroom. Together we see it every day.

Christ said something similar: "Do not worry about tomorrow, for tomorrow will worry about itself. Each day has enough trouble of its own" (Matt. 6:34).

Live day by day, receiving the good with thanksgiving and coping with the evil by God's gracious power. Remind yourself every day that God in Christ forgives your failures and accepts you as you responsibly confess those failures.

God may not like failure. God, however, loves failed people. God does not will losses upon us. God, however, continues through thick and thin to love losers.

And if God chooses to bring success to you and through you to others, take joy. When God brings you wisdom and strength through your losses, take joy also. And God will resurrect you all and bring even a secular society to a sacred conclusion.

That is God's job—in Christ. Praise him!